H

Crime Scenes

Paranormal Evidence From Crimes & Criminals Across the USA

Mark Nesbitt
&
Katherine Ramsland

Table of Contents

Introduction

In *How to Think Like Sherlock Holmes*, Maria Konnikova, describes how the iconic detective honed his mental process into a precision machine. What characterizes Holmes's approach, she says, is a "natural skepticism and inquisitiveness toward the world." Yet Holmes was also alert to errors of thinking from subconscious influences, such as the tendency to see what we want to see and the pressure from our desire for closure.

We appreciate Holmes's perspective for ghost hunting as well. We've seen "errors of thinking" among people in the paranormal world. We also appreciate that Holmes's creator, Arthur Conan Doyle, believed in the paranormal, which suggests that even within Holmes's rigor, there's still room for things not easily explained.

That's why we start this book with Sherlock Holmes. He offers some wise precautions.

"A fool takes in all the lumber of every sort that he comes across," he tells Watson, "so that the knowledge which might be useful to him gets crowded out ... so that he has difficulty in laying his hands on it. Now the skillful workman is very careful indeed as to what he takes into his brain attic."

Posing the limited diffuse mindset of Dr. Watson against the fluid empowering mindset of Holmes, Konnikova addresses how mental laziness steers us away from the hard work of examination and reasoning. Our minds are made to wander, she states, and we prefer to let them go. But this is no way to think like Sherlock Holmes. If we want his powers of perception and cognition, we need the "two

Ms"—mindfulness and motivation. In other words, think ahead, clarify your end point, be prepared for options, and develop an effective distancing device.

That's what we try to do as we explore this second volume in our paranormal forensics series. In *Blood & Ghosts*, we looked at the tools of paranormal and forensic investigations and described how these approaches complement each other. We consulted with former FBI profiler Gregg McCrary and described examples of good investigations, as well as those that contained errors.

Although we devoted a chapter of *Blood & Ghosts* to haunted crime scenes (and will repeat several here with expanded ideas), this book looks at different types of haunted crime scenes, murder implements, victims, crimes with supernatural components, and related investigations. This book focuses more on the paranormal phenomena at crime scenes (places more than process), adding the results of our own investigations in some and offering suggestions for paranormal forensic investigation in others. Sometimes, we just want you to enjoy the story.

The Haunted Crime Scene

People have asked us whether all crime scenes are haunted. Our sense of this is that they probably are, but we're concentrating on those where psychic or paranormal phenomena have been reported—especially by several unrelated people. In addition, not all haunted sites are crime scenes, so unless there's some indication that a natural, accidental, or suicidal death is something else, it won't be included.

An example would be the death of Marilyn Monroe. A psychological autopsy was done to fully investigate her death, but so much information has emerged in subsequent years that there are plenty of questions and this incident is worth revisiting. Maybe it was a murder, but maybe it wasn't. Since it's unclear that her death was a suicide (the official finding), we'd consider this an appropriate case for this book. Because ghosts sightings have been reported in her former Brentwood home, it *could* be a haunted crime scene. Plus, her ghost has reportedly been seen in Hollywood Westwood Memorial Cemetery, where she's buried, and the Roosevelt Hotel.

If we were to investigate this incident, we would want to find out what are the ghost reports, and was the psychological autopsy correct and complete?

At the age of 36, Monroe was found dead in her bed. On the bed stand were empty bottles of recently filled prescription drugs, and given her general emotional instability and trouble with depression, it seemed like a clear case of suicide. However, more than four hours had passed between the housekeeper discovering her and the call to police. In addition, Monroe's body appeared to have been posed and the housekeeper was doing laundry when the police arrived. Investigators thought that these were troubling behaviors.

Deputy Medical Examiner Thomas Noguchi performed an autopsy and found that Monroe had died from acute barbiturate poisoning, specifically an overdose of Nembutal and chloral hydrate. He sent samples of several of Monroe's organs to the toxicology lab, but they dropped the ball and performed only a partial analysis (a blood and liver test). Believing the case was closed; the technicians destroyed the untested organs. Due in part to this, as well as to resistance over the idea of suicide from those who knew Marilyn, rumors began to swirl that President John Kennedy and his brother were implicated—especially when Monroe's diary went missing. It wasn't long before conspiracy theories arose that Monroe had been murdered and a cover-up (including the death investigators) was underway.

The coroner gathered consultants, which the media dubbed a "Suicide Panel," because they were the city's suicide specialists. They spoke with Monroe's agent, former husbands, business associates, friends, housekeeper, and psychiatrist, as well as all of the investigators involved. They looked specifically for factors that indicated that Monroe was capable of suicide and had been depressed recently. Ultimately, the panel concluded that she fit the profile for suicidal depression. She'd been fired from a movie set, gone through three failed marriages, had a drug addiction, had two devastating miscarriages, and serious attachment issues from having a severely mentally ill mother. She'd overdosed before on a drug that one must take in large quantities to be fatal. In addition, the door and window to her bedroom had been locked from the inside.

Yet Monroe also had reasons to live. She'd made significant plans, and many who saw or spoke to her during the day before she died had seen no sign of depression. Those who knew her well were aware of how often she forgot which drugs she was mixing with liquor. To them this overdose seemed accidental rather than suicidal. Even the psychiatrist who came to her home that day and spent several hours with her was not convinced of suicide.

Noguchi was mystified when the case was reopened twenty years later, because he thought his procedures were beyond reproach. He admitted to puzzling elements—notably the lack of drug capsules in Monroe's stomach—but had decided that her stomach had pushed the pills into the intestines, which had not been properly examined. However, he did not explain why she was found neatly laid out in bed rather than in the sort of convulsed position that an overdose tends to cause, nor why so much time had passed before the authorities were called.

Marilyn Monroe's death still attracts theories about political conspiracy. In 2005, a former Los Angeles prosecutor, John Miner, who'd been present at the autopsy, revived notions about murder after he revealed a secret he had carried for years. Monroe's psychiatrist, Dr. Ralph Greenson, had allowed Miner to hear tapes that Marilyn had sent to him of their therapy sessions. Miner had heard nothing on the tapes that supported a finding of suicide. He'd taken extensive notes.

However, as more information has emerged, it seems clear that Monroe had a disturbing habit of attempting suicide and requesting help, mostly for attention. In light of revelations over the past decade that have contributed to a more comprehensive psychological autopsy, it seems most likely that she accidentally took a fatal overdose and failed to call for help in time.

There's nothing unusual about her ghostly appearance, except for the fact that it seems to hang out for no reason at the Roosevelt Hotel's pool. She has appeared in a full-length mirror in her Roosevelt Suite #1200 so often that guests complained and the mirror was moved to the lobby. A photo taken by a guest in the ballroom showed an anomalous light reflection that resembles the face of a beautiful blonde. Monroe's distinctive figure has also been observed outside her former home and at her interment site in Hollywood's Westwood Memorial Cemetery.

Perhaps she was just not ready to go.

In the pages that follow, we'll look at other cases like this, and when we can, we'll add relevant investigative angles from paranormal and forensic arenas.

We'll rely on the Conan Doyle/Holmes method of inquisitiveness, skepticism, careful analysis and awareness.

Paranormal Forensics & Investigative Tools

Although this book in our series is focused on places more than procedures, let's quickly review some tools.

Forensic Investigation

The following should be on every investigative checklist, forensic or paranormal:

1. **Identifying information:** Location, date, time, and names of participants

2. **Information about the Scene:** A basic description of the scene and incident, as well as whether it was immediately secured against contamination

3. **Scene Processing:** Whatever was recovered, its location and description, as well as time and circumstances of recovery

4. **Items Processed at Scene:** Blood, fingerprints, liquid or dry substances

5. **Photo/Video/Audio Log:** Types of photos, videos or audios, with conditions recorded

6. **Analysis:** Immediate impressions and ideas, as well as fraud detection

7. **Potential Methods:** List and description of usable methods for investigation.

Problem solving during investigations of any type consists of trial-and-error, rule-based approaches, sudden insight, and heuristics ("rule of thumb" shortcut strategies). We tend to limit ourselves to the perceptual habits we develop, known as our mental or perceptual sets. Thus, we're prone to confirmation bias, in which we recognize and accept those things that support our biases and ignore counter-evidence. This is endemic in investigative work and can produce significant errors. So can the precise way in which we focus attention. It's important for investigative consultants to stay up-to-date on cognitive discoveries. For example, the highly touted gut-instinct can easily lead investigators into error, but few people know about the factors that make it unreliable. They prefer to accept the "shortcut" sentiment, "Trust your gut."

"Cognitive mapping" is a concept that describes how we become habituated to a specific perspective. It goes by other names, like a cognitive model, a mental map, a script, or a frame of reference. We encode, recall, and recognize our "situated existence" according to familiar parameters. That is, we learn things from our families, associates, and culture that become integrated into our personal interpretations. How we physically and emotionally process the world within our cognitive maps guides our decisions, interpretations, and behavior.

We mentioned earlier about how cognitive errors can influence forensic investigations. Gut-instinct, especially, can result in what's called a threshold diagnosis, which can be quite superficial and block out important items for a fuller analysis.

(Note: "Gut-instinct" is what many people believe psychics use when "reading" a scene. Observing psychics at work will tell you that, instead of a "gut" instinct, their actions appear to be more of an intellectual exercise than anything involving instinct. "Intuitive" is probably a more accurate description of how psychics operate.)

With training and effort, investigative decision-makers can improve the intuitive system. Complex tasks such as a criminal investigation should be undertaken carefully, with eyes and mind open. Suggested strategies for defusing the potential negative impact of heuristics and cognitive errors on investigative tasks (and this goes for any type of investigator) include:

- Teach investigators about the impact of cognitive heuristics on their work.
- Teach investigators how to form and analyze competing hypotheses.
- Create a case-specific checklist of key assumptions.
- Spell out areas of uncertainty or ambiguity as attractants for heuristics.
- Demonstrate a "devil's advocate" approach and its value.
- Examine the impact of ego investment and fatigue on focus and thinking.
- Practice being mindful and aware: observe and think about details.
- Resist pressure to conform to groupthink.
- Study *good* investigations to learn the benefits of observational alertness and mental flexibility.

For example, after the double homicide of Nicole Brown Simpson and Ronald Goldman, paranormal researchers claimed to have photographed their images in the leaves of trees at the scene. To some extent, this can be explained by a human perceptual process known as pareidolia or apophenia, in which the brain forms patterns from random stimuli. But for the sake of argument, let's take it seriously as a paranormal event. The deceased Simpson and Goldman paranormally formed the leaves into the features of their faces. What might we bring to it, forensically?

Paranormal Investigation Basics

To watch one of the "ghost hunting" shows on TV might give someone the wrong impression as to how a crime scene can be investigated paranormally to gather additional information.

First of all, it is not necessary for a Paranormal Investigator (P.I.) to work only at night. Ghosts do not have to wait until night to emerge and share their information with the living. Mark has collected well over one thousand stories from various observers and they are split, predictably, down the middle: half occurred during the daylight hours. So, statistically, there is no ideal time to attempt to gather additional information from the other world on a crime that occurred in this world.

In addition, there seems to be an over-emphasis on scientific gadgets, meters, hacked radios and so forth. It is important to remember, there is no such thing as a "ghost detector." Detecting equipment only identifies when an anomaly is present in the environment.

Equipment can be separated into four categories, although there may be some overlap:

1. Detecting
2. Recording
3. Communicating
4. Analyzing.

Since one theory concerning the nature of ghosts indicates that they may be the remnants of the electric charge the human body possesses during life, some detecting equipment consists of Electromagnetic Field

Detectors like K-2 meters, Mel-meters, compasses, and other magnetic devices that indicate the presence of an electromagnetic field. As well, a drop in temperature, perhaps caused by the spirit's need to draw energy from its surroundings, is historically associated with a ghost's presence. Quick-read thermometers, infrared thermal scanners and non-contact thermometers detecting temperatures at a distance are other pieces of equipment used to detect paranormal activity.

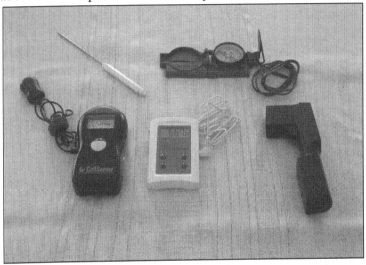

Detecting Equipment

Once paranormal activity is detected, the investigator must record it for analysis later. Historically, cameras have been used to record the evidence of ghosts. (Unfortunately, photographic evidence was sometimes faked.) The current breed of digital devices—both still and video cameras—are excellent for a number of reasons. First, they are relatively cheap to purchase. Second, they are cheap to operate; multiple exposures can be made of a single scene without the cost of reproducing them on paper. Finally, most digital photographic equipment is small, lightweight and extremely transportable. Unless you wish to make it a profession, with high-end infrared "FLIR" cameras, most people can afford and already own the kind of cameras acceptable for ghost hunting.

Audio equipment can be classified as both recording and communicating equipment. Tape or digital recorders can be used to record anomalous noises during an investigation. They can also be used to ask questions of the spirits in the hope of getting information via EVP or electronic voice phenomena. EVP is the recording of words or phrases not necessarily heard by the investigator. Pertinent questions about the site, its history, or the spirits involved, can sometimes be answered in this manner. At a crime scene, a dead victim, witnesses, or even the perpetrator could be addressed using this technique.

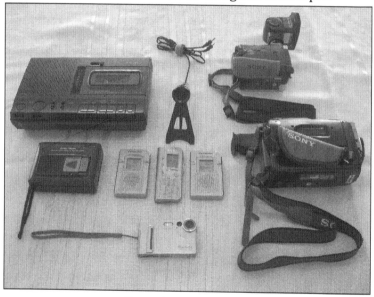

Recording Equipment

Once information is gathered, it must be analyzed. Home computers now come with software that allows you to enlarge investigation photos for analysis, or to slow down videos for closer inspection. Audio software to graphically analyze sound recordings is also available. Computers have the ability to store and transfer this evidence for others to analyze.

But with all the high-tech equipment and its emphasis on TV shows, it is easy to overlook the most sensitive and sophisticated piece of equipment available: the researcher himself.

A quick read thermometer is slow compared to the human skin when it comes to detecting a cold spot.

The classic indication of the presence of a ghost—one's hair "standing on end"—may merely be the electromagnetic charge being detected by the investigator.

When investigators have "that feeling" that something is amiss, it may be the intuitive sense that something in their surroundings is of a paranormal nature.

Some investigators—particularly mediums—can actually see spirit energies. An analysis of Mark's collected ghost stories indicated that a classic ghost sighting is very rare. Only about 10 percent of his stories involve visual manifestations of ghosts. But nearly all the other senses are involved in detecting ghosts.

Over 60 percent of Mark's stories consist of auditory evidence of ghosts, the sound of footsteps being the most common. People have smelled out-of-place odors like decomposition where bodies were once gathered for burial, rotten eggs on a battlefield where black powder propellant's main ingredient was sulfur, and cigar or pipe tobacco where no one is smoking.

Paranormal investigators have been touched by ghosts, pushed by ghosts, and seen items moved by ghosts. All these manifestations do not need equipment to be detected.

Psychometry is a method wherein a sensitive holds an object and gives her impressions of what the energy of the object contains. At a crime scene where some objects such as a weapon, a victim's clothing or an object that was present while the crime was committed are supercharged with remnant energy from both the victim and perpetrator. Information can be gleaned from that object.

Remote viewing, developed during the Cold War, is a technique wherein trained individuals see a distant scene, perhaps even into the past, and pass on information from it, such as who is present.

Psychics can be brought into a crime scene to give their impressions: names, descriptions of participants in the crime, weapons used, hiding places and locations of weapons or perpetrators can sometimes be discerned.

Paranormal investigators can use pendulums or dowsing rods to get names or find burial sites. Mark's wife Carol has located gravesites with dowsing rods at several Civil War battlefields and an abandoned churchyard in Virginia—apparently we leave remnant energy behind even when our physical bodies are exhumed.

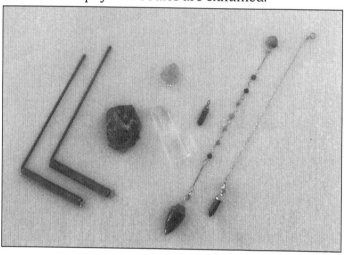

Pendulums and Dowsing Rods

While not necessarily admissible in court yet, findings from paranormal sources can at least give crime scene investigators new leads to follow.

Photonics: Digital Facial Recognition

Facial recognition technology is now crucial to investigations. We can use software for matching face imagery acquired from video or still cameras with face-recognition databases. The face is mapped with digital dots to turn it into something like a fingerprint—uniquely identifiable. Suspects can even be identified just by their gait caught on camera.

For example, counterterrorism officials would use facial recognition software to try to match faces of possible suspects with faces in databases of images from passports, visas and driver's licenses. During the Boston Marathon bombing, hundreds of photos and videos were studied for this purpose, frame by frame.

There are also developments in fusion techniques that will make storing and transmitting facial images much more efficient. One system employs multichannel image fusion for 3-D color face imagery. The keys to accuracy include improved resolution, advances in algorithms for effective matching, and better computational power. When images are enhanced with digital technology, it's possible to see more in them. You can even calculate their changing emotions and their pulse from one photo to the next.

When the FBI released blurry, off-angle images of the two primary suspects in the Boston Marathon bombings, researchers with Carnegie Mellon University's CyLab Biometrics Center worked on them to improve the focus. The scientists digitally mapped the face of "Suspect 2," turned it toward the camera, and enhanced it to make it matchable in a database. Authorities were able to identify him as Dzhokhar Tsarnaev, a student at the University of Massachusetts, Dartmouth. Under controlled conditions, when the face is angled toward the camera and if the lighting is good, the accuracy of this technology has been as high as 99 percent.

Cyber experts believe it's only a matter of a few years until computers can identify almost anyone instantly. Computers could then use electronic data to immediately construct an intimate dossier about each of us. From an image of a face, its match will be found in a database of driver's license portraits and photos on social media sites. From there, the computer will link to the person's name and details such as his or her Social Security number, preferences, hobbies, family and friends.

Recently, a supposed ghost image from 1995, believed to prove the existence of an afterlife, was debunked using photo facial matching. Tony O'Rahilly had taken photos of a fire ravaging a town hall in England. When he looked at them later, he claimed that he'd captured the image of a little girl surrounded by flames.

This became known as the "Wem Ghost," and many believed that it was 14-year-old Jane Churm, who reportedly had started a fire in that town in 1677. However, more recently, Brian Lear found a 1922 postcard from the same town that looked remarkably similar to her, right down to the dress and bonnet. This pretty much discounted the "spirit photo" as genuine. The story was a fraud.

Photography experts suggested that the technique used was likely similar to what the Edwardian Age mediums used to "capture" images of spirits during consultations. The mediums would first ask for a photograph of the decedent so they could impose it onto a glass plate. Later, a picture would be taken of the client using this same glass plate, which showed the decedent's image as a "spirit" hovering over his or her loved one. This fraud played on people's emotions. They wanted their loved one to appear, so they believed that it had happened.

Unmasking a sophisticated forgery can require an expert. However, efforts to automate the detection of doctored images and make these processes more accessible are achieving success. For example, Fourandsix Technologies began selling an add-on for Photoshop, called FourMatch, which determines whether an image has been manipulated. It compares the "metadata" associated with the image against a database of signatures that represent characteristic ways in which different devices capture and compress image data. Since this program cannot yet determine the difference between a slight tweak and a significantly changed photo, it still requires a human interpreter to see inconsistencies in shadows, reflections and incorrect perspective.

For digital photography, the JPEG Format Analysis algorithm makes use of information stored in meta-tags from JPEG files. These tags contain information about quantization matrixes, code tables, and many other parameters. The content and sequence of those tags, as well as precise tags available, depend on the image itself, the device used, or the software that modified it. These tags also show ambient light levels, shooting conditions, the camera model, color profiles and other such information. If a JPEG file has been edited and saved, certain compression artifacts would appear.

A common practice performed by those who fake images is to lift and transplant parts of the same image across the picture. For example, the background from one area can be "cloned" to patch another area. To detect this, we identify image blocks that look artificially similar to each other.

Fraud analysts use a comprehensive software solution that implements algorithms based on statistical analysis of the image information. Most alterations performed on JPEG files can be detected right away, especially by those experienced with how images can be altered.

Another way to see if an image has been manipulated relies on the camera's grid of light sensors. Of the millions available, several are usually flawed, and these flaws produce a slight discoloration that repeats across photos. If the pattern of unusual discolorations in two pictures taken by the same camera match, then neither has been retouched in those areas.

How to Fake a Ghost Photo

Katherine attended a crime scene photography workshop for digital single-lens reflex cameras and heard the term, "painting with light." After several hours spent on other techniques, the instructor addressed this intriguing concept.

The first step was to create a scene, so one of the workshop participants laid down on the floor to simulate a body. The others set up the cameras on tripods, because a key requirement is that the cameras remain absolutely still. The camera also had to be capable of being set for a long exposure time.

The second step was to have a nice, bright flashlight ready. Some crime scene flashlights provide a lot more light than a typical flashlight. This instructor had one from Sirchie, a crime scene investigation supply company.

When the "body" was in place, the "photographers" stood next to their cameras. The lights were turned off, and there were no windows, so the room was pitch black. They opened the shutters for a 30-second period and stood back.

The instructor moved his flashlight over the body several times. He lit up the scene that the photographers would capture. Once the shutter stopped, they looked at the resulting photos. Katherine was astonished to see a photo as if it had been taken in good light. The point of this for crime scene photographers is to be able to take photos in dark places, such as poorly lit basements or wooded areas where there is little to no light. But she also noticed something else.

In some of her photos, there were streams of light similar to what she'd seen on many ghost photos. She also noticed that a shot she had taken of several men standing in the dark looked absolutely ghostly, as if they were transparent.

With this technique, you can use the light like a broad brush, or you can use it as a pen for more precise results. If you move the light slowly over your photographic subject, you'll get better results, unless you hold it too long, which "burns" it.

Katherine observed that someone who knows this technique would have no trouble recreating photos to show off as ghost photos. Being aware of this technique gave us yet another tool for investigating fraud, which is all too rampant in the ghosting-hunting community.

Fake Ghost Photo

Yet even without fraud, we can imagine that many of the results that amateurs get are probably similar to this technique. They just don't realize it. To them, getting strings of light or luminous images in a dark place couldn't be explained by camera work alone. Yet, just moving the camera a bit in the dark will get some of these effects.

In fact, the participants in the workshop were quite surprised by the results of painting with light, despite being experienced photographers, because they'd never tried it before. If *they* were mystified, we can see how ghost hunters would be doubly convinced that the images that emerge from the dark could only be paranormal. Care must be taken.

Remote Profiling

In *Blood & Ghosts*, we described how the FBI conducts psychological profiling. Briefly, behavioral profiling uses information from a crime scene (or series of scenes) and crime documents to devise a comprehensive set of personality traits and behavioral probabilities to help narrow the potential pool of suspects. An elite unit at the FBI, formed during the 1970s, has made the process famous, but it's been in use since at least 1888 with the crimes attributed to Jack the Ripper.

The word 'profile' has picked up different meanings over the past two decades, so we'd like to sort through them to clarify what we mean.

During the 1990s, members of the FBI's Behavioral Science Unit (BSU, now called the Behavioral Analysis Unit, or BAU) began to write and publish books about profiling. While Robert Ressler was the first to publish, it was former BSU chief John Douglas who brought the greatest visibility to the subject with his international bestseller, *Mindhunter*. His basic philosophy is that people are slaves to their personalities and offenders will thus leave a pattern of clues at a crime scene from which their traits and behaviors can be deduced. That is, one can "profile" (a verb) in order to develop a "profile," (a noun). The point is to narrow the pool of potential suspects. This gives us two definitions for 'profile.' But there are more, which has resulted in some confusion.

The idea of "reading" crime scene behavior caught the public's attention and the media began to misrepresent the concept. Journalists talked about "the profile of a serial killer" as if it was an *a priori* blueprint that offered a checklist for a type of offender rather than being the analysis of behavior specific to a crime scene (or set of scenes). In other words, many reporters and news anchors spoke as if the list of traits for a perpetrator of a specific type of crime was already mapped out, so that we could measure suspects against it. So now we have two meanings for the *noun*: a pre-crime portrait and a post-crime portrait.

Unfortunately, some investigators adopted this erroneous notion and have mistakenly dismissed suspects who failed to fit the serial killer prototype. Many scriptwriters like this version as well.

Assuming that we have enough behavior in current databases for devising prospective blueprints, they still only work for categories of offenders who operate in similar ways, such as disgruntled middle-aged mass murderers who commit workplace violence or healthcare serial killers. Despite the many generalizations made about serial killers, there are too many differences from case to case, especially in other countries, to use a checklist-based profile.

In a book by Ronald and Stephen Holmes about criminal profiling, they use "profile" in yet one more way. They criticize Special Agent Russ Vorpagel for failing to predict the suicide of Richard Chase. In other words, they assume that profiling is a risk assessment. But it's not.

This error brings us to a yet *fifth* notion of profiling: that it means "reading" people the way Sherlock Holmes would do in a Conan Doyle story. In other words, profilers supposedly possess the keen ability not just to interpret behavior at a crime scene, but they so fully understand human nature that from only cursory observations they can lay out the rich details of someone's life story.

So, with retrospective profiling in mind (a verb), we've coined a term that meshes this procedure of analyzing crime scenes with remote viewing, to get "remote profiling." In other words, to devise a solid profile, one needs a crime scene or crime scenes photos, plus other data. If you add the enhancement of a remote viewer, you can "visit" the crime scene without actually going there.

A quick reminder: although remote viewing has a long history among shamans as a specific form of real-time clairvoyance, more people know about the CIA program developed during the 1970s-1990s, as "psi research" for spying capabilities. This began at the Stanford Research Institute, a California-based think tank. SRI researchers had experimented with various forms of paranormal skills and had settled on clairvoyance. They sought real-time sight at a distance as the most practical skill to develop, but they did venture into seeing into the past and future (with apparent success). They expected to be able to send their mental vision through all barriers, no matter how thick or strong. They also wanted to dissociate themselves from 1960s "Age of Aquarius" touchy-feely concepts, so they switched from the word clairvoyance to remote viewing. The Army adopted this as well.

Science writer Jim Schnable documented the Army's experiments in *Remote Viewers: The Secret History of America's Psychic Spies*. He makes the technique sound strikingly impressive, as if these guys were wildly accurate when, in fact, only a couple of them became the regular go-to guys. The program also relied on outside psychics, only one of which stuck with it for any length of time. Still, they did demonstrate the viability of this skill. Despite some claims that this technique requires a great deal of mental discipline and practice, several beginners were able to perform remarkably well with only minimal training. (One woman who came to debunk the program was able to "hit" three times out of three, so she became a member of the team.)

Several men from Army Intelligence were screened for their sensitivity and trained at Fort Meade. The test was simple: set up a remote target, like a specific building or a garden, and send a person out to it. Then find out who could accurately reproduce it by seeing through his eyes without laying eyes on it themselves. Later, they just used coordinates on a map, without sending anyone to the target. But the exercise that involved an outgoing person ("outbound remote viewing") also produced other sensations, such as taste, smell, and the feel of the atmosphere. (In one case, an outbound agent stopped for a chocolate bar and the remote viewer tasted it, too.) The viewer would go into a deep trance state and would either sketch what he or she saw or just write a description. Usually, they did this in a fairly dark, quiet and isolated room. Typically each viewer had a monitor who knew what the target was and who could then ask more specific questions if the viewer was getting it right.

Traits found to be associated with talented viewers were artistic ability, creativity, and visual-spatial skills. They were also good at describing scenes. Even better, they had an interest in the paranormal world and perhaps some psi experience from earlier in their lives. Some had an enhanced sensitivity to human targets, i.e., a missing or injured person. A few could see auras, the subtle fields of energy around a living body.

Long-established, fixed targets were easier to view than moving or temporary targets. It turned out that seeing numbers and letters clearly was one of the most difficult tasks, often impossible. (Thus, they never won the lottery, and also could not locate rumored buried treasure.) One of the most difficult tasks was to search for someone at an unknown location. If the viewers tried moving their hands across a map, they got poor results. And there were burnout problems. Doing this activity excessively seemed to dry up whatever brain networks they relied on. They experienced a barrier that they couldn't get past and they would feel emotionally fragile.

The best results occurred if there was feedback on their success, boosting their confidence. As they worked at it, these elite viewers believed that anyone could learn how to do this. However, they had few examples to confirm this theory.

One of the most successful remote viewers in this program was an outside psychic, Patrick Price, who had some investigative experience as well. Another was Joseph McMoneagle, designated #001, because he was the first to be recruited to the SRI by agents from the Department of Defense. Apparently, there was sufficient success for this program to last for over two decades in the military.

However, there certainly are misses (errors) or cases that show no real progress. On McMoneagle's website, he describes working on a cold case that involved the son of a real estate developer from Beverly Hills, California. The son murdered the father by tying him to a chair and stabbing him with a bowie knife. He placed the body into his car and parked it at a Los Angeles airport before fleeing the area. So, there was no mystery as to the victim or the killer. However, the police wanted to locate the son.

McMoneagle took on the case with a retired detective from the LAPD, Jimmy Sakoda. They worked on it for a year, tracking the killer to Oregon, but there they lost the trail. McMoneagle offered a description of an area that appeared to be in Vancouver, Canada. On the website, it says, "It turned out that many of Joe's sketches and drawings strongly matched the Richmond neighborhood of that island area. Many of Joe's drawings matched in nearly perfect detail the downtown and harbor areas, and even some of the more specific general-use public buildings that the man they were hunting might have used or occupied— such as the interior of the main or downtown public library building. The neighborhood area in which the search finally settled turned out to be so unerringly accurate when compared to Joe's drawings, Jimmy was able to stake-out a particular duplex building in a specific parking area."

However, there was no evidence that the man they were looking for was there. In fact, they did not catch him. Had this all worked the way it was presented in Schnable's book, there should have been quick results.

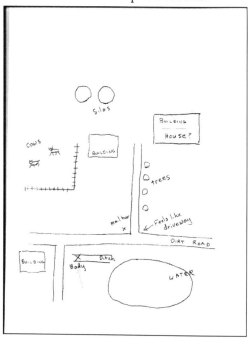

Sample Remote Viewing Map

It seems that a person does not have to be highly trained or specially gifted to remote view, although, as with everything else, practice can improve results. At a conference in Gettysburg, Pennsylvania, Mark Nesbitt and Laine Crosby challenged the participants to remote view a site they were to visit later that afternoon. Most drew general sketches, several were completely off base, but sisters Holly Martin and Colleen Keller drew remarkably detailed sketches of the farm they were to visit. Their perspective was from the porch of the house, including the overhang with a door on the small barn, the pond, and even the underground streams that fed it. The drawings made by trained remote viewers published in books on the subject were often mere lines or simple geometric designs.

To add some science into this subject, we're aware of some interesting work done recently with rats at Duke University that might shed light on how remote viewing can work.

A rat in a cage in North Carolina was teamed up with a rat in a cage in Brazil. Both went through a series of training phases. The leader rat learned to use a lit light bulb to choose one of two levers to press. Electrical signals from the "leader" rat's brain were collected and encoded. These signals were then sent electrically to the follower rat's cortex. This rat had been trained to receive and act on electrical stimulation. The follower rat would press one of two levers in response to the signals from the leader rat, getting rewarded for a correct choice. The leader rat eventually learned that the clearer he was with his "instructions," the better his chances of getting a double reward. It's a case of conditioned learning, but the rats are nowhere near each other. The researchers believe that humans, with their greater sensitivity, would do even better.

A recent study, funded by the U.S. Army Research Office and other non-military federal agencies, a professor of computer science and engineering at the University of Washington sat in his lab on August 12, 2013, wearing a cap hooked up to an electroencephalography machine. He watched a computer screen while he mentally played a simple video game. At one point, he imagined moving his right hand to fire a cannon. The EEG electrodes picked up the brain signals of the thought and transmitted them to a man across campus wearing a purple cap with a transcranial magnetic stimulation (TMS) coil placed over his left motor cortex (which controls movement of the right hand). When the first researcher had the thought to move his hand, the second one involuntarily moved his right index finger to push the space bar on the keyboard in front of him. It felt, he said, like a nervous tic.

So, back to remote profiling: It's a talent of developed skill that acquires information from places or events at a distance, not visible to the viewer. The remote viewer might be given coordinates of a crime scene or series of scenes and asked to produce drawings or written impressions. These could be compared against crime scene photos.

This approach could still prove useful for locating missing persons, although we've already noted how much more difficult it is to remote view when the geographical target is unknown. We can think of no better case on which to apply it than the recent case of a serial killer.

Israel Keyes, a 34-year-old Anchorage construction worker, was picked up in 2012 in Texas for the kidnapping and murder of a 19-year-old woman, Samantha Koenig, in Alaska. He'd kidnapped her from her job in a coffee shop, raped and strangled her, and left her body in a shed while he went off on a cruise. Two weeks later, he took a photo of her to make her seem still alive and demanded a ransom. Then he dismembered her and dumped her into a lake. He withdrew funds from a designated bank account, jumping from Alaska to Arizona, New Mexico, and Texas. He made some mistakes and was finally brought to ground.

Keyes admitted to the murder and told investigators where to find Koenig's dismembered parts, which they located. During his interrogation, Keyes also confessed to a double homicide of an older couple in Vermont, and added that he had killed even more people. Police suspected that he began his killing spree about ten years earlier. He named New York and Washington State as places where he'd killed, but he declined to give specific details until law enforcement would agree to meet his conditions: keep his name out of the media and give him a speedy execution.

As the process dragged on and seemed to become one-sided, Keyes stated, "The problem is, I don't have any typical demands. There's not anything you can offer me at this point and I realize that now."

When it appeared that prosecutors might not keep their end of the bargain, Keyes committed suicide in December 2012. He provided no further victim names or details in his rambling suicide note. Investigators now have little to go on.

Keyes had been a careful predator. He'd scouted locations and buried his murder kit (knives, ropes, chemicals, zip ties) in various isolated places long before he committed any murders. He wanted to ensure that he did not make the same errors as his murder mentor, Ted Bundy. Whenever he got in the mood to kill, he would travel to some remote place and find victims near his stash. He'd use zip ties to bind them.

Keyes had partially funded his attacks with bank robberies, because he didn't want to leave a paper trail with credit card receipts. He told investigators that he'd looked for victims in remote locations, such as parks, campgrounds, trailheads, cemeteries and boating areas.

Officials now seek the public's assistance to learn if Keyes was seen where people turned up missing. Although there is as yet nothing paranormal associated with this case, a paranormal method in another case offers possibilities. In the following case, searchers successfully used remote viewing. We described this in *Blood & Ghosts*, but it's worthwhile to repeat it here.

In 2006, Steven B. Williams, a Denver-based DJ, was missing. A friend of his, photographer Robert Knight, had not heard from him in a month. Knight turned to Angela Thompson Smith, who had worked with Princeton Engineering Anomalies Research team (P.E.A.R.S.) and founded the Nevada Remote Viewing Group. She gathered a retired airline captain, a civil engineer, a former Air Force nurse, a civilian Air Force contractor, a librarian, and a photographer.

Each was given a coordinate on which to focus. Each member undertook one to three hour-long sessions. They were shown a photo of the missing man, but received no other information. During the session, they formed images of a body in water near Catalina Island off the coast of California. They thought it was caught in some netting.

On the same day they gave Knight this report, a body was found off Catalina Island. Knight called the morgue. He offered several identifiers, which matched the John Doe, and Williams officially became a murder victim.

The group also did a viewing of the suspect. Knight was aware of an investment advisor named Harvey Morrow, who had befriended Williams. He'd invested money for Williams, but then had disappeared. So had the money. So, the remote viewers went to work again. One of them sketched a boat with Morrow on board, and they thought it was somewhere in the British Virgin Islands. Morrow was in fact in the Caribbean. When Morrow went to Montana for a job, his boss learned that he was wanted in connection with a homicide. He was arrested and later convicted.

So, to look for potential victims of Israel Keyes, the investigation must begin with his own descriptions of his modus operandi. We have a number of items that can assist: remote locations, possible use of bankcards or accounts, bank robberies around the time of someone disappearing, and possible communications to victim's families for ransom. This involves what the FBI calls linkage analysis with behavioral evidence. However, without more details, it's impossible to use the FBI ViCAP database.

Since Keyes was uncommunicative in life, it is likely he will be uncooperative in death. The attempt to get EVP will focus on the victims, possibly in the location of their deaths when known. Questions to victims to elicit a description of their killer could be useful. General locations or GPS coordinates can be given and the remote viewer can supply details of the site.

On Monday, August 11, 2013, the *Anchorage Daily News* and other media outlets ran a feature on a report released by the FBI, and this provides more useful data.

Reportedly, Keyes suggested that there were victims in ten different states. The following details were in this report:

During either the summer of 1997 or 1998, Keyes grabbed a girl floating on the Deschutes River in Oregon on an inflatable tube. He lived in Maupin, OR at the time, and the abduction is thought to have occurred near there. It was late afternoon or early evening and the girl, described as between 14 and 18, was with friends. He sexually assaulted her and let her go. She did not report the assault (and still has not, despite all the publicity).

Keyes joined the Army in 1998 and was discharged in 2001, when he began living in Washington State. He told investigators that he'd killed a couple in Washington sometime between 2001 and 2005. He might have moved the couple's car and he alluded to having buried them near a valley.

In either 2005 or 2006, during the summer or fall, Keyes killed in two separate encounters. He tied four or five milk-jug anchors to at least one of the bodies, which he dumped in Washington's Crescent Lake, leaving it in more than 100 feet of water. He used his boat to dump another in water, but it is not known where.

Keyes moved to Alaska in 2007, driving north on the Alaska-Canada Highway. He flew to Seattle on Oct. 31, 2008 and traveled to multiple other states. He rented a 2008 PT Cruiser in Seattle, then flew from Seattle to Boston on November 2.

Keyes admitted to burying a cache of money and guns near Green River, Wyoming. Known dates of travel to the Wyoming area are September 2007, July 2008, and September 2011. He also buried a cache near Port Angeles, WA, but it's not known when he did this.

Keyes admitted to abducting and killing a girl or woman in an East Coast state April 9, 2009, and robbing a bank the next day. This might be the girl he described as having pale skin and a wealthy grandmother. She was driving an older model car. (However, this could also be another victim.) Keyes told investigators he crossed multiple state lines to bury the body in upstate New York, and then robbed Community Bank in Tupper Lake, N.Y., on April 10. After the bank robbery, he parked for several hours in a nearby campground outside of the area. He was registered at the Highlander Inn in Manchester, NH, for a week.

From July 9 to July 12, 2010, Keyes went on a trip to Sacramento and Auburn, California, renting a black Ford Focus. He drove about 280 miles in those three days.

Keyes flew to Chicago on June 2, 2011, and drove to Essex, Vermont, where he abducted and killed Bill and Lorraine Currier on June 8. Afterward, he drove around the

East Coast before returning to Chicago. He then flew to San Francisco on June 15, stayed the night there, and returned to Anchorage the next day. (The Curriers bodies were never found.)

On February 1, 2012, Keyes abducted Samantha Koenig, raped, and strangled her and dumped her dismembered remains in Matanuska Lake near Palme, Alaska. He went on a cruise out of New Orleans and came back through Texas. The FBI believes he killed someone at this time. He set fire to a home in Aledo, Texas, on Feb. 16 and robbed National Bank of Texas in Azle.

Three days before he killed himself, Keyes seemed concerned about a Cold Steel Tanto 4.5-inch folding knife that was missing from his girlfriend's house. He hinted that investigators might find evidence on it associated with one of the Washington State murders. It had not been used to kill the victim but might have been used to dismember.

Keyes traveled internationally and it is unknown if he committed any homicides while outside of the United States. He described several trips to Montreal. In addition, on his way to Alaska in 2007, Keyes drove alone through Canada.

We invite readers to attempt to remote view for this case. The more minds at work, the better. You can find our email address at the end of this book.

Haunted Crime Scenes Across the USA

Arizona

Overcrowded Bungalow

Katherine went to college in Flagstaff, where the Monte Vista Hotel houses several entities. Built in 1927, this place became a second home to many actors who were shooting films in the canyons and deserts nearby. A phantom bellboy, a wounded bank robber, and some murdered prostitutes are among the legendary spirits. But she found a much more interesting haunted crime scene in a neighborhood near the Northern Arizona University campus.

Friends of Katherine, Crissi and Don, described their experience in a small rented bungalow on North Agassiz that had been built in the twenties. (We withhold addresses for private residences.)

"It was a snug little home," Crissi said, "with a sunroom, hardwood floors, a claw-foot tub, and a backyard for our dog, Bagheera, a 110-pound German shepherd/Akita mix. Upon arriving, we took the dog into the house. He walked ahead of us, sniffing the sunroom floors, and then approached the living room. About halfway through, he stopped, whined, sat down, and would not move. It took us five or ten minutes to drag him out to the backyard. We attributed it to the new surroundings.

"However, four months later, I was sitting on the couch watching TV. Bagheera was dozing on the floor in front of me. Suddenly, he jumped to his feet and looked at the ceiling. Within seconds he was whimpering and cowering on the floor while crawling backwards out of the living room. He kept his eyes on the ceiling until he got to the hallway. I froze and stared at the ceiling, trying to see what it was that frightened this normally bold dog. I tried coaxing him back with me. He crouched down and looked at me, still whining and refusing to come back. This made me doubly nervous.

"I called Don and he said there was probably a squirrel in the attic, but I didn't think a squirrel would cause that much fear in a big brave dog. By the time I was off the phone Bagheera had rejoined me. I shut off the TV and looked at the ceiling, poking at it with a broom handle, trying to see if anything furry was indeed making its home in the attic. I heard nothing.

"Not long after that, my husband and I woke up to the sound of the plastic divider doors between the main rooms rattling violently. Our first reaction was that someone was trying to get in. But Bagheera hadn't warned us. Don got up and as he got out of bed the rattling stopped. We both wondered if our snug little home might be haunted. It always felt crowded."

Don's side of the story was even more dramatic.

"In the middle of the day," he said, "I was walking through the kitchen to the backyard. Off of the kitchen was a doorway to the spare bedroom. As I passed through I glimpsed out of the corner of my eye a young boy of four or five with brown hair. He was standing next to the bed in the spare room with his hand on the bedpost. I stopped and did a double take, but he was gone. Soon after that I started seeing lights flashing in the night, similar to flashbulbs on cameras.

"Then one evening I got up to go to the restroom, which was located off of the spare bedroom with a door that also went into the living room. As I opened the door to return I encountered a wall of white light that filled the doorway. Instantly all the hair on my body stood on end. The cold in the air was not normal.

"Soon after these experiences I asked our landlady if the house was haunted and she said that once, while waiting for some prospective renters, she'd used the restroom and an elderly gentleman and the young boy walked through two closed doors. She admitted that a family had moved here from California and the father couldn't find work. Soon after arriving in Flagstaff, he killed his wife, son, and father, and then turned the gun on himself."

After that, Crissi consulted an herbalist who told her to smudge the house with sage and cedar during the full moon and for ten more days. "The smudging seemed to help," she said, "and the house felt less crowded, but the incidents kept cropping up."

Although Katherine did nothing further on this property at the time, it would have been a simple matter to look up newspaper archives to learn about the incident—to ensure it wasn't just folklore. If that could be established, the next step would be to get the police report and possibly to interview relatives who might have known the family. For paranormal purposes, the sightings are interesting and this seems like a prime property to set up cameras and to attempt to get EVP. If the story is true, a lot of people died violently in this small house.

Haunting in Tombstone

Considered to be among the most haunted areas of the American Southwest, Tombstone, Arizona, is the site of the infamous gunfight at the O.K. Corral. The sudden violence from that fateful day seems to have left some residual energy behind.

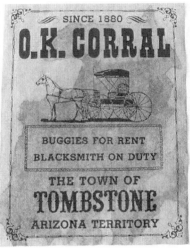

The Earp brothers had come to the lawless town of Tombstone in 1879 to get rich from silver mining. Virgil Earp became a deputy marshal and then served locally as the town marshal, while Morgan Earp assisted him. They were asked to go after the Cowboys, who'd robbed many stagecoaches and disturbed the tenuous peace between Mexico and the U.S. by rustling cattle and killing Mexicans.

During this time, Wyatt decided that he wanted to be sheriff of Cochise County, which sparked animosity between him and the current Sheriff Johnny Behan. Wyatt then made a move on Behan's wife, Josephine. A feud soon developed between the Earp brothers and the sheriff, who'd befriended the Clantons, rumored to be members of the Cowboys.

The Cowboys grew more violent, so the marshal in Prescott, Arizona, asked Virgil Earp to arrest them. He deputized Wyatt, Morgan and Doc Holliday to help him confront the Clantons.

On the afternoon of October 26, 1881, the Earps and Holliday armed themselves and went over to the corral. They approached via an adjacent vacant lot. Virgil charged five men at the corral, two of them Clantons, with the illegal act of bringing handguns into the city limits. They heard the click of guns being cocked. Someone, possibly Wyatt, opened fire.

In the next thirty-one seconds, Ike Clanton and another Cowboy fled, and the others started to shoot. Doc fired at Tom McLaury, hitting him in the gut. Virgil and Morgan shot at Billy. Frank went after his horse as he held his stomach wound closed, while Tom collapsed and died against a telephone pole. Morgan took a shot in the shoulder from Billy, and Morgan shot at Frank, shattering the top of his skull. Billy fired at Doc, hitting his gun holster. Billy fired at Virgil and hit him in the leg. Wyatt and Virgil shot back, killing Billy. Wyatt was the only one to escape unscathed.

According to historians, the Tombstone city fathers considered the gunfight an outright homicide and Virgil was fired. Then Morgan was murdered two months later so Wyatt went after three other men in revenge. To avoid being arrested, he then fled to Colorado.

But something remained behind from that day. It's said that several people have seen the figure of Billy Clanton walk across the corral, a troubled soul, both victim and perpetrator. Others have reported spirits that they associate with the Earp brothers, although none died there. This might be what we call a "residual haunting" or place memory—an image apparently stuck in time, repeating itself on occasion.

Also in Tombstone is the Birdcage Theater, a bullet-riddled Old-West saloon that has stood in place since 1881. According to the History Channel's "Haunted Tombstone," a jealous woman murdered another who was flirting with her man by using a stiletto to cut out the offending woman's heart. The victim is among the reported 31 spirits that haunt the place. With at least 26 deaths in the building, that's no surprise. The former saloon is now a museum, and staff members have reported seeing apparitions. People have heard the ghostly echoes of music and laughter both inside and outside.

Even the streets of Tombstone, formerly scenes of frequent violence, are haunted. Residents and tourists alike have seen a former madam, reportedly hanged in her nightgown, and a man dressed in fancy western gear leaning against a post.

The Superstitions

Curtis Merworth, 49, was intrigued with tales of gold supposedly hiding in the Superstition Mountains east of Phoenix, Arizona. A resident of Salt Lake City in 2010, he invited two friends to join him on an expedition to get rich. They acquired a treasure map from a Native American that they believed would lead them to the Lost Dutchman Mine. However, the area reportedly was cursed. Thus, this incident has paranormal overtones.

The curse is traced back the early 1500s, when Spanish Jesuit priests built missions in the territories of Arizona and New Mexico. They established relations with Native Americans, who helped them mine gold. When the priests were ordered back to Spain in the late 1700s, they convinced the locals that bad things would happen if they ever revealed the mine's location.

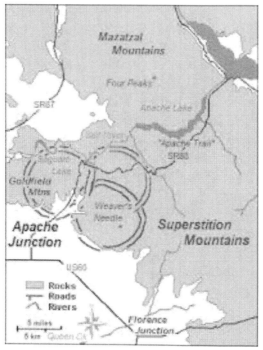

Fabled as a mother lode mined by a Mexican family in the 1840s, it was supposedly discovered during the 1870s by Jacob Waltz, a German immigrant. Waltz brought a partner, whom some unknown person murdered. Waltz purportedly hid stashes of gold before returning to Phoenix, where he died in 1891. One legend says he revealed the mine's location on a map, but over 100 searchers have died trying to find it.

Merworth had already attempted a journey into the Superstitions on his own, but suffered from dehydration and had to be rescued. Apparently, he thought it was safer to take some friends. For his next attempt, along came Malcom Meeks, 47, and Ardean Charles, 66.

They packed sleeping bags, food and six jugs of water. Strangely, they did not take a cell phone. Apparently, they planned to return at the end of each day to their motel. Still, this truly was odd: Merworth had survived the first trip only because he was able to call for assistance. What were they thinking? Had the curse clouded their cognitive abilities?

Even worse, in 2010, they set out in July, typically the hottest month for Arizona. The temperatures often reach well over 100 in that desert climate. These men were not only ill prepared; they were hardly in shape for such an arduous hike into a place where dozens had disappeared. The 160,000-acre wilderness area is filled with steep canyons, rocky outcroppings, cacti and heavy brush. Two of them even had medical conditions. Curtis's mother had a premonition and begged him not to go. She was certain she'd never see him again if he did. But he was determined to find the Dutchman's lost gold.

As predicted, the three men did not return. A week went by. Their vehicle was located at the trailhead to the Lost Dutchman Mine State Park. Curtis's mother saw more terrible images of them stuck and unable to get help. Officials and volunteers from Maricopa and Pinal Counties made over twenty searches for six days with no success. The soaring temperatures prevented them from going out again. Most believed that the men had to be dead from the heat. The search was finally called off.

Six months later, in January 2011, a man familiar with the area went for a hike. He stumbled upon two sets of decomposed skeletal remains, encased in clothing. There were shreds of black hair on one and gray on another. He noticed that one skull had two holes that looked like bullet holes and that the ribs seemed to have been kicked in.

Dental records confirmed that the remains were Meeks and Charles. Searchers went out again and discovered scattered bones and ID about a mile away. This was believed to be Merworth's remains.

The official cause of death for all three was exposure. Only the man who discovered them has talked about the holes in the skull. There is no evidence that law enforcement ever followed up. However, there's a story from the 1930s of an earlier prospector whose skull was found with two bullet holes, so perhaps this man confused the two tales.

Also, the documentary on which he was interviewed mentioned that the man who'd given Merworth the map came to a bad end: he fell into a viaduct and died. Apparently, the curse caught four in its net. The news greatly disturbed the parents of another treasure hunter who'd been missing since 2009.

Jesse Capen, 35, had consulted more than 100 books and maps before plotting his path. He left supplies in a hotel room, with the intention of returning to retrieve food and water on weekends. Yet, once this Denver hotel bellhop set out, he quickly vanished.

Three years later, hikers came across Capen's Jeep, wallet, backpack and cell phone. Not far away was a boot that led to a set of human remains. The body was in a crevice roughly 35 feet up a cliff face in the southern portion of the Superstition Mountains.

A trail of evidence suggests that Capen died on December 4, 2009, the first night of his trip, before he even had a chance to unroll his sleeping bag. In 2011, hikers had found a note in a metal can atop the peak that said: "Jesse Capen was here. Dec. 4, 2009." Searchers had focused on 4,892-foot Tortilla Mountain, but failed to find him. The 2012 discovery of remains gave his parents hope.

The skeleton was large, and Jesse had been 6 feet 4 inches tall. His parents recognized the teeth they'd paid dentists to repair. The boots and clothing matched as well, and in 2013, DNA confirmed it. Capen had been just half a mile from his camp when he fell off a cliff. Despite all his preparation, he never even got a start.

The treasure continues to elude those who set out to find it.

Florida

A pair of restaurant owners seeking a larger space for their business at Church Street Station reneged on a contract to rent some property in Orlando, Florida. They claimed the building was haunted. The area was originally a train depot that had become derelict and was taken over, renovated, and transformed into a premiere shopping and entertainment complex. Allegedly, the ghosts of murdered children haunt the place. As the legend states, they were born to prostitutes over a century ago and were killed on the property.

The building's landlord filed a lawsuit against Christopher and Yoko Chung; the parties who'd reneged on the contract, because extensive renovations had been done for them. The landlord even offered to have an exorcism performed, but apparently this was not enough. The Chungs' attorney claimed that they'd said that construction workers had reported seeing the ghosts. They contended that the landlord had not disclosed this, and the Chungs' religious beliefs forbid them from having any association with spirits of the dead.

Besides the sightings of apparitions in this building, people have reportedly heard a piano playing although no one can find it. A ghost tour starts here.

*　　*　　*

In West Park, Florida, Henriette Lubin, 57, was attacked in her home, which caused neighbors to ponder supernatural possibilities. Lubin had lived in the Lake Forest Section. On Monday night, May 8, 2006, around 10:00 P.M., neighbors heard screaming. It was Lubin's daughter, Martide, who'd just found her mother's body. The police were called and within a few minutes a number of patrol cars arrived. They discovered that Lubin's car, a 1995 Nissan Maxima, was missing. Ms. Lubin had last been seen earlier that evening, so when her daughter discovered her dead, the murder was clearly quite recent. The police would not give out details, except to say there were marks of trauma on the body.

Eerily, it had also been on a Monday night, seven years before that the bodies of two people living in the same house were discovered. On May 4, 1999, John and Mary Holzknecht, ages 78 and 77, were brutally murdered. Apparently their young neighbor, 17-year-old Joseph Cotto, had been in a "killing mood," as reported in the *Miami Herald,* and had invaded their home, stood over them as they slept, and slashed their throats. He then used cologne to cover the smell of blood on his hands. As an afterthought, he stole some credit cards, a small amount of money, and drove their car to South Beach. When he was caught, he pled guilty, receiving two life terms.

Add to these incidents a third scenario at this address more than two decades earlier (some sources indicate it was only a few months earlier): the elderly couple's 30-year-old mentally ill son had committed suicide there. Given a suicide and a double homicide, the house had gained a bad reputation, but Henrietta Lubin, a former crossing guard, had purchased it anyway, the year before she died.

Neighbors who spoke to reporters claimed that the house was "evil," "bad," "wrong." Relatives of the elderly couple suggested that there was a terrible presence there. The next-door neighbor said, "There is something very peculiar about that house. I think it's haunted. They need to tear it down."

Georgia

Savannah Businesses

The Shrimp Factory opened in 1977, and its owner has been convinced ever since that it is haunted. The center of seemingly paranormal activity is an upstairs room used to store liquor and wine. Employees often report hearing strange noises coming from this room. No one knows for sure what the source is, but some say a man died there from a heart attack, while others attribute the restlessness to the brutal way that slaves were treated in a former time. The building itself dates back to the 1800s, when slaves were bought and sold. They brought cotton in to the warehouse and were chained to the wall upstairs to prevent them from escaping while their masters were busy elsewhere. Some died from exposure or illness. They wouldn't have called this murder, but it was certainly homicidal neglect. Employees who go to the upper rooms report strange feelings, and some hear voices calling to them.

*　　　*　　　*

Photo Courtesy of Shannon Frost-Holzemer

There's also the Moon River Brewery, formerly the City Hotel. As a hotel, it housed a rough-and-tumble crowd of river men who drank heavily, played cards, and frequently quarreled. In 1832, a fight began when Dr. Philip Minis beat the hot-tempered James Jones Stark fair and square in a card game. But Stark wasn't happy. He growled out loud for others to hear that he wanted to kill Minis. In fact, he let his loss simmer into nasty racial slurs, and finally Minis requested that Stark apologize. Stark refused, so Minis' friends urged him to defend his honor. On August 9, 1832, Minis challenged Stark to a duel, and Stark readily accepted. His unusual choice of weapons was rifles.

They met at a common dueling area on the Savannah River, but Minis requested a delay in the hope of persuading Stark to accept the more traditional pistol as the dueling weapon. Stark went to the chosen spot by himself and fired a rifle to symbolically claim his victory. He then went back to town and ran into Minis at the corner of Bull and Bay. Their respective friends prevented a clash, but the men came together the following day in the City Hotel.

Although the Anti-Dueling Association had attempted to intervene, it was too late. Anxious to end the entire affair, Minis unbuttoned his coat and reached for his pistol. Declaring Stark a coward when Stark came down the steps, Minis fired. The bullet went directly through Stark's neck. Minis was arrested and arraigned. After a two-hour deliberation, the jury acquitted him.

Apparently, Stark was unhappy in the afterlife as well, and many people think he haunts the place. Some claim they feel a push or shove as they're coming down the very stairs he took to meet Minis. Others say they've heard the crack of the pistol and the rattling of glasses. Still others claim to have witnessed men carrying Stark's body outside on the back of a door.

*   *   *

The centerpiece in Isaac's at #9 Drayton Street is the bar, which was built in England in the 1700s, disassembled, and shipped to Grand Central Station in NYC. It came to Savannah in 1920. The building now houses a British-style restaurant/pub.

One of the most famous ghostly encounters is the story of "The Hanged Man," Bud "Brute" Bailey. Visiting from Britain, he challenged Jack O'Dwyer, an Irishman who lived in Savannah, to a bare-knuckle fight. But things went wrong. Jack fell twice, but always managed to get to his feet. Then Bailey punched him hard several times in the face. O'Dwyer died from his bludgeoning. The spectators, friends of O'Dwyer, grabbed Bailey and called him a murderer. They forced a noose around his neck and hanged him in the back room of the old pub before burying his body in the cellar. They pledged to keep the secret and just say that Bailey had run away.

This wasn't just a tall tale, either. Many years later, a body that resembled Bailey, as he'd been described, was unearthed during an excavation. The coroner said he had died from a broken neck. Ghost stories hold that the shadowy figure of a hanged man can sometimes be seen in the cellar. People have also heard a man's sharp cries.

*   *   *

Of the two adjoining houses that comprise the Foley House, Dr. Lewis Knoor built one in 1868. Honoria Foley, the widow of a wealthy Irish immigrant, Owen Foley, completed the other in 1896. Owen and Honoria Foley had married in 1850, when he was 40 and she was 20. Owen died five years later, leaving Honoria and their two children his considerable estate. However, due to the Civil War and its aftermath, the assets were frozen, so Honoria took in lodgers. She thus became the first Foley House innkeeper.

One of those boarders, a wealthy exporter, disappeared in the middle of the night and was never heard from again. In 1987, during a renovation of the Foley House, skeletonized human remains were found in a wall between the two houses. Although the remains were never identified, legend has it that this was the missing boarder, who may have been murdered for his money. Or, he was a dishonorable man who entered Honoria's room one night to have his way and received a clunk on the head that killed him. She then engaged the brick mason to help her get rid of the body. Since he was a traveling salesman, everyone thought he'd merely departed.

The inn's staff often hears stories about sightings of a man in a top hat walking around in the garden in the late evening. Others report a sudden chill near where he was once entombed.

Ghost Abodes

A short walk east from the Foley House is a tiny cottage painted "haint blue," a color that legend holds will ward off spirits. (The blue color is like water, which some legends say that spirits cannot cross.) A female bar owner had lived in the cottage. Her husband had jilted her, running off, and she became bitter about men. In fact, she was once arrested for assault against one of her male customers. For the rest of her life, she refused to allow men into her house, and this apparently continued even after she died. Her cottage was left to a relative, who either ignored or did not care about the former owner's anti-male ban. She rented the cottage to a man.

On his first night there, he claimed that he'd felt a pair of small hands around his neck, trying to strangle him. The second night passed without incident, but on the third night, he felt the hands again, so he moved out. Another man tried it, but had a similar experience, so thereafter, as the story goes, the landlord decided to rent only to women. This is one of the few ghost stories that, if true, involved a ghost in an attempted murder. In fact, nearby is a house with a similar tale.

*   *   *

At 507 East St. Julian Street, the Hampton-Lillibridge House is often referred to as Savannah's most haunted house. As a result of briefly living here, the infamous Jim Williams (*Midnight in the Garden of Good and Evil*) developed a keen interest in psychic phenomena. He kept notebooks on many different subjects in this area, including voodoo. This house was his second restoration in Savannah.

Built in 1796 by an architectural firm from Rhode Island, it had deteriorated during the early twentieth century, serving as a rundown boarding house. Reportedly, a depressed sailor had hanged himself from a brass bed frame in one of the rooms. In 1963, Williams purchased it and moved it four blocks from Reynolds Square to its current location. In fact, a worker was killed during this transition when part of the roof of a neighboring house collapsed. Williams hired a crew to begin work, but they started having strange experiences. They heard footsteps, voices, laughter, mumbling, and the sound of furniture being thrown around. When they were working on floors in the basement one night, they heard the sound of several people running up and down the steps, but no one was there. A news crew caught wind of the rumors and entered the unoccupied house one evening. They saw a piece of construction material come flying at them.

One of the scariest incidents involved a man who went to an upper story to investigate a loud noise in a room that was supposed to be empty. When he failed to return, others went to find him and discovered him lying facedown on the floor, shaking. He was terrified. He told them he'd walked into the room and felt as if he had plunged into ice-cold water. He seemed to lose control of his body, which was being drawn by a force toward the open chimney shaft, so he had dropped to the floor. This, he believed, had saved him from being pushed to a thirty-foot drop, four floors below, to a concrete slab. The others thought the house should be exorcised, but when they discussed it, they heard a loud female scream coming from somewhere in their midst, as if a woman stood right there among them.

Workers also reported seeing a tall man dressed in black with a silver cravat glaring at them through a third-floor bedroom. Some passersby had spotted a gray-haired man wearing a silver morning robe on a day when Williams had left and locked up the house, and neighbors often heard party noises and a woman singing. Once they reported seeing people dancing on the top floor when the house supposedly was empty. Lights turned on and off when no one was home, and a maid told Williams she was afraid of a male presence she sensed inside. Hearing chairs moving around, she'd fled.

Initially, Williams dismissed the idea that his new house was haunted, although he was aware that an empty crypt had been found on the lot. Eventually, he moved in. Several times he was awakened by the noise of footsteps in his room, like someone crunching broken glass underfoot. He saw a dark figure approach him and disappear. He chased another figure down the hall until a door slammed in his face. He found it locked. He was finally willing to acknowledge that something odd was happening. He was ready for an exorcism.

Williams invited an Episcopal bishop, the Reverend Albert Rhett Stewart, to perform the exorcism. On December 7, 1963, the holy man walked through the entire house, blessing it and commanding the evil presence there to leave. However, his rituals apparently failed because within a week the noises returned.

Hans Holzer, an investigator of paranormal phenomena, came in and assured Williams that the house was certainly haunted. Other psychics sensed a female presence, including one with children. The American Psychical Research Foundation in North Carolina investigated, and they, too, affirmed the phenomena, as did a team from Duke University, hired by subsequent owners.

Savannah Haunts

Colonial Park Cemetery is the final resting place for many of Savannah's earliest citizens. Among them is Button Gwinnett, a signer of the Declaration of Independence who was mortally wounded in a duel. Also, more than 700 victims of the 1820 Yellow Fever epidemic are buried in Colonial Park Cemetery, as well as victims of Savannah's tragic dueling era. Savannah history records the first dueling death in 1740 and the last one in 1877. Local historians estimate that some 10,000 bodies are buried in and around the park, although presently the cemetery has only about 600 marked graves.

The cemetery was closed to burials before the start of the Civil War, but the war did leave its mark. Federal troops occupied the cemetery grounds, looting and desecrating many of the graves. They even removed bodies to sleep inside vaults, and there are rumors that, as a practical joke, Union soldiers changed the dates on many of the headstones.

The Colonial Park Cemetery is also home to one of Savannah's most famous ghosts, that of Rene Asche Rondolier (or Renee Rondolia Asch). He was a disfigured orphan, some seven feet tall, who made his home among the vaults during the early 1800s. (One account said he had parents but they made him play in the cemetery so he could avoid the other children.) Often the butt of jokes from other children, he kept to himself as much as he could. When pets went missing or were found dead, people blamed Rene.

Colonial Park Cemetery

Then one day the bodies of two children were found on the grounds. A mob formed and came after Rene. They dragged him to a nearby swamp and hanged him. When the body of another child, as well as a woman, turned up in the cemetery, many believed that Rene's ghost had done it. However, it's more likely that this proved they had lynched an innocent man.

Many say that Rene's ghost still wanders through the cemetery at night. Or, if someone sees a ghostly figure, it could be the spirit of the man in the following tale.

After 11:00 P.M. on November 16, 1901, Samuel T. Baker, a 62-year-old Confederate veteran, was on his way home from a late night at the accounting firm where he worked. He had deposited his paycheck, spoken to his son-in-law, and withdrawn a dollar to take care of some errands. Near his office, Samuel passed a fruit stand. He spoke briefly with the fruit vendor and mentioned that he was going to stop and get a shave. On East Broughton Street, Samuel stopped in at Gayou's Barbershop. After his shave, he bought a bottle of whiskey for a friend and started home fifteen blocks away. He decided to cut through the cemetery.

A half-hour later, three young boys walking through the burial ground found him barely alive and lying in a pool of blood. His skull had been smashed and his eyes were badly bruised. He could barely make himself understood. The boys ran to the police station near the northeast corner of the cemetery.

The desk sergeant dispatched two officers to investigate. The boys led them to the injured man. The officers saw his bottle of whiskey, now broken, and assumed they had another drunk. Over his mumbled protests, they dragged him to his feet and threw him into a cell. He received no medical attention.

When he didn't show up, his son-in-law, E. M. Hopkins, went looking for him. Entering the cemetery, he spotted the blood and broken whiskey bottle. He walked quickly back to the office. He also found the people who had last seen Samuel, but he didn't find Samuel anywhere. Recalling the blood, he stopped at the police barracks. They affirmed that they had Samuel in custody. Hopkins convinced them to put his father-in-law into his care and he took Samuel home.

As the family cleaned him up, they realized that he'd been hit twice in the head, cracking his skull. Sometimes he mumbled something, but they couldn't understand what he meant. "Leave my clothes and shoes," he said. "There are two to one. Please leave my clothing." By early morning, Samuel was dead.

Several theories were floated, and the last one anyone believed was the police theory of public drunkenness. Samuel was a reliable, respected citizen. He had no history of a drinking problem. Clearly, he had been attacked and murdered. Many believed it had been a botched robbery, and while his pocket watch was missing, he still had the change in his pocket left from his errands.

Another theory holds that a policeman beat him up and the others covered it up. Samuel Baker's granddaughter, Marie Hopkins Steadman, claimed one day that she knew who it was. Although she maintained until her death in 1999 that the killer had finally made a deathbed confession, she never revealed it.

Some people claim to have seen a figure in the cemetery that resembles Samuel T. Baker, with his turn-of-the-century clothing and handlebar mustache. In fact, they have seen what looks like blood running down his face from an apparent head wound.

Ghost Tour

There are a number of haunted crime scenes within walking distance in Savannah's historic district.

At 421 Bull Street on the west side of Monterey Square is the famous red brick Mercer House. General Hugh Mercer, the great-grandfather of singer Johnny Mercer, initiated its construction in 1861. However, no Mercer ever lived in it, as the Civil War interrupted the building and afterward Mercer sold the house to another family. During the early 1900s, a Shriners' organization took it over and it eventually came into the hands of Jim Williams, who was a private restorationist. He'd already renovated a number of historic homes and had turned his eye toward the Mercer House. It took him two years to restore it, and thereafter he used the spacious carriage house for his international antiques restoration business. He enjoyed playing the fine southern gentleman until the day in 1981 when he shot a young hustler who lived with him named Danny Hansford.

Mercer House

Williams's fame spread from Savannah around the world, due to John Berendt's bestselling "nonfiction novel," *Midnight in the Garden of Good and Evil*. It inspired a film directed by Clint Eastwood and starring Kevin Spacey as Jim Williams. By this time, Williams himself was dead. The reason he gained such notoriety was because the evidence contradicted his claim of self-defense. He was indicted for murder.

First, let's consider the Mercer House itself. Williams's philosophy was, "If you like it, buy it," and what he purchased revealed his taste in European antiques, oil landscapes and portraits, and refined décor. One item that jumps out is an iron sculpture of the "Four Horsemen of the Apocalypse," precursors to the world's end. In addition, Williams had collected paintings of birds of prey, specifically vultures and falcons. Draped over the back of the couch in the vulture room was the preserved head and skin of a jaguar. Williams was not a hunter. He just liked predators.

Each year Williams threw a socially significant Christmas party, but this tradition ended when he killed Danny, his lover and "part-time assistant." Starting in July 1982, Williams went through a historic series of four trials. New evidence surfaced from witnesses who stated that Hansford had planned to harm Williams, so during the fourth trial in 1987, he finally won an acquittal.

Just eight months later, Jim Williams died, some sources say from a heart attack, some from pneumonia. He had just turned 59. Some whisper that Danny's ghost, unhappy that justice had not been done, extracted revenge. Scenes from the book and movie indicate that his spirit remains restless. A few years after Williams's death, people who'd come to view the Mercer House on the anniversary of his annual parties reported that they had seen the house ablaze with lights and alive with the sound of revelers. However, there have been no parties in this house since Williams died. Those who have visited Danny's grave have gotten EVP on a recorder. A remote viewing psychic told one visitor that Danny was seeking revenge.

*   *   *

In *Midnight in the Garden of Good and Evil*, the author, John Berendt, did not specify an address for where this next story took place, but Jim Williams mentions that it was "one square away" from where he resided in the Mercer house. This incident happened during the 1930s. The son of a judge was seeing the girlfriend of a prominent gangster. He was ordered to steer clear of her, but he refused. The next thing the family knew, this guy was left on the front porch, bleeding badly, with his genitals tucked under his lapel. He was taken to the hospital, where he died. The family told the press that he'd merely fallen from the porch.

*   *   *

Yet one more haunted crime scene south of the Old Colonial Cemetery is 432 Abercorn Street, on the east side of Calhoun Square. The house has seen several deaths, including a disturbing triple homicide.

The house was built in 1868 for General Benjamin J. Wilson, a veteran of the Civil War. The General's wife succumbed to yellow fever, leaving him to raise their daughter alone. She loved to play with children who went to Massey School, but her father disapproved. Undeterred, the little girl continued to run across the street, so, according to the legend, he tied her into a chair in front of the window. She could do nothing but sit and watch. Eventually, she died from heat exhaustion and dehydration.

In 1959, a family visiting from Florida stayed in this house. They had four daughters, ranging in age from four to twelve. The adults went out one evening, and when they returned they found three of the girls dead. Two were still inside the house, and one was sprawled on the front porch, as if slain while trying to escape. The youngest daughter, age four, was the only one still alive, but she was unable to describe what had happened. The sad and senseless triple murder was never solved, but female ghosts are sometimes seen in this house.

*   *   *

Wright Square, at Bull and President Streets, was laid out in 1733. During Savannah's early days, a pretty girl named Alice Riley emigrated from Ireland. She became a bonded servant to William Wise, a cruel and sadistic master. Her one consolation was that she married the plantation's butler, Richard. She told him she was forced to do things with Wise against her will, which angered Richard, so they formed a plan. In March 1734, while Alice was bathing Wise, they drowned him and fled to the Isle of Hope. However, they were captured, brought back, and sentenced to die. Alice insisted she was innocent. She was also pregnant, probably with her master's child, so she was forced to watch Richard be hanged in Wright Square. After the baby was born a few months later, Alice had her turn on the same hanging tree on January 19, 1745. Her body remained there for all to see for three days.

Her ghost is one of the most frequently reported in the area. She runs through the square in tears, screaming for her baby. In addition, no Spanish moss grows from the tree on which she was hanged, a sign that she might have indeed been innocent. Reportedly, the police have received calls from tourists who claim to have seen a frantic woman looking for a lost baby. No one blinks at her period costume, since the historic district has so many guides in costume.

Idaho

Double Trouble

The Lewiston Civic Theatre, at 805 Sixth Avenue in Lewiston, Idaho, is housed in the historic Bollinger Performing Arts Center, named for the famous opera singer, Anne Bollinger. A native of Lewiston, she gained an international reputation. The theater has been in this gothic stone structure for over thirty years, and once shared the building with a church. This didn't protect it from a killer.

In 1982, about ten years after the theater moved into the building, two girls were murdered. Then, no one saw the janitor again, so he became the prime suspect. The murder went unsolved, and as with many such incidents where closure proves elusive, the spirits of the dead appear to dwell in the place.

The youngest of the victims has been seen climbing the stairs. One or the other might also show a mischievous side. They don't seem to be seeking their killer or even trying to get attention to their unsolved murders. Instead, they merely show up from time to time, perhaps a reminder of whom they once were.

The apparition of a jilted bride has also been spotted walking between the rows of seats. As with most haunted theaters, there's always someone who just loves the theater and lingers after death to watch the shows. Some people believe this woman is the spirit of a former director.

One website indicates that some 70 spirits—all allegedly harmless—haunt the place. Peculiar incidents occur, such as a trap door that opens and closes without assistance from human hands, lights that go on and off when no one's there, and candles that flicker out on their own. Even the chandelier gets into the act with an independent spin or two.

Susan Engle wrote about the place while on a quest to experience a ghost. She claims that after six years of dogged ghost hunting, she has failed to track one down. She and her cohorts even spent the night in the Lewiston Civic Theatre.

"It was creepy and fun all at once," she says, "skulking around in the nether reaches of the old building and poking about in places not normally open to the public. Was it haunted? Not that I could tell. I never saw a ghost, heard disembodied whispers, or even felt a chilly frisson of dread and unease creep up my spine."

New Jersey

At 217 South Street in Morristown, New Jersey, is a mansion that has changed hands many times. When

Katherine visited, it was a restaurant named Jimmy's, but is now (according to Google Maps) a TD bank branch.

As the story goes, John Sayre built the place in 1749 for his family, and it was peaceful until 1833, when Samuel Sayre hired an immigrant sailor, Antoine Le Blanc, to be a handyman. By some accounts, Le Blanc got greedy and by others, he was in love with Sayre's daughter or maid, who resisted him. In any event, one night, he used a shovel to murder the Sayres and an ax to kill the maid, Phoebe. He then took what money he could find and fled.

But it wasn't long before a posse hunted him down. They brought him back to Morristown and put him on trial. This event reportedly drew thousands, as did his hanging after he was convicted. A couple of scientists were allowed to experiment on the body. They applied electricity to try to reanimate it. Failing this, they turned the corpse over to the tanner.

Since people were so eager to have some part of this offender, the town officials decided to skin the culprit and sell pieces of his hide. People purchased them to make into wallets, purses, and lampshades, and some of these items can be viewed today at the Morristown Museum. (We're not sure if any are haunted.)

Eventually the home was bought and converted into an eating establishment. In 1957, a fire burned it nearly to the ground, but it was eventually restored. When it became the Wedgewood Inn, the stories about spooky events proliferated. The room known as Phoebe's room seemed always to be a different temperature than other areas, usually colder. (When Katherine visited, it was warmer.) Some waitresses caught Phoebe's reflection in a mirror, and one reported seeing a bloody hand reach out from one of the paintings. Things would be moved around or simply taken. People would feel hands on their shoulders, but find no one behind them. In addition, after closing for the night, which involved extinguishing candles on the tables, the staff would often look through a window to see a candle or two lit again.

At one point, the restaurant became Society Hill, and the owner boldly decided to inaugurate it on the anniversary of the tragedy. On the night of the grand opening, a punch bowl cracked open and broke, spilling its contents all over the table and floor.

Some psychics have indicated that LeBlanc and Phoebe both exist in the place as restless entities. They've tried to exorcise the spirits, but cooks and wait staff continued to describe eerie sensations. One waiter told Katherine that an unseen force had spun him fully around.

It's not known whether bank personnel have experienced anything unusual there.

New Mexico

La Casa Vieja de Analco is reportedly the oldest house in America. More interesting to us is that, under certain conditions during the early morning hours, a decapitated ghostly head supposedly rolls down the street outside. Why it's there is an interesting tale.

The two-story adobe building is at 215 East de Vargas Street, near the Old Santa Fe Trail, in Santa Fe, New Mexico, and it rests on the former foundation of a Native American pueblo that dates from around 1200 AD. The word "analco" means "across the water." The tribe remained there for nearly two and a half centuries before it moved south. In 1598, Don Juan de Onate led a party of Spanish settlers into the area. With him were Tlaxcalen warrior auxiliaries. They liked the area, but were eventually driven out during the Great Pueblo Rebellion of 1680. The Pueblo people took over the buildings. Around 1709–1710, the "Oldest House" became the temporary residence of the Spanish Territorial Governor.

"Oldest House"

During the past century, the house has been used for various commercial enterprises, such as a coffee shop, museum, and curio shop. At one point, someone set what was believed to be the mummified corpse of an old Indian named Geronimi in a chair in the back room. People would place coins in his hand, apparently for luck. It turned out that the mummy was actually a medical model, dressed in Native American garb to attract tourists. Still, a legend says that an old Indian did die in the house during the 1920s and some visitors claim to see him in the back room.

According to the legend, some time during the late seventeenth century, a man named Juan Espinoza asked a pair of herb women, or *brujas*, who lived in the Oldest House, for a love potion. He paid the bill but the potion didn't work, so he wanted his money back. They refused. He grew angry and threatened them with his sword. They ended up decapitating him. Although accused of murder, they never went to trial. However, they kept Espinoza's decapitated body. Supposedly, they took this corpse with them when they eventually vacated the house.

Today, amid all the historic relics and antiques, you can see a coffin-shaped box containing something that certainly looks mummified. A colorful blanket lies on top of this coffin, just short of where the head would be, and a plaque explains the tale of Juan Espinoza.

No one seems to know why he haunted the place in the form of a rolling head. Apparently, it shows up on the anniversary of his death, but since we don't know exactly when this occurred, it's difficult to verify.

Ghost Ranch

Katherine went on a pilgrimage to Ghost Ranch, where the reclusive American artist Georgia O'Keeffe lived a solitary life. O'Keeffe had purchased an adobe home on this

22,000-acre former cattle ranch in northern New Mexico because she fell in love with the barren landscape.

Ghost Ranch

This place wasn't always called Ghost Ranch, and the reason it has this name today depends on which story you want to believe. They all come back to a pair of early serial killers. Thanks to them, the place was named el Rancho de Los Brujos, or the Ranch of the Witches.

According to a book by Lesley Polling-Kempes, during the late 1800s, this area 15 miles north of Abiquiu began as a homestead to take advantage of the drought-proof Rito del Yeso spring, one of the few water sources in this otherwise arid place. The Archuleta brothers claimed a large tract of land for raising cattle and built several primitive cedar structures. One had a wife.

Other cattlemen came through and sought hospitality. Usually, they disappeared and their herds were sold to enrich "Los Animales," as the brothers were called. Often, they didn't wait for "guests" but went out looking for cattle to grab. With little law enforcement around and most people afraid of the brothers, they got away with murder and thieving for years.

Stories circulated about missing people whose items were seen in their possession, and if history is to be believed, they became quite successful and prolific as serial killers of the American West. Tales arose about bodies thrown into unused wells or people pushed to their deaths off the high cliffs.

It wasn't long before ghost stories followed. Some described the sound of the wailing voices of murder victims on the Ranch of the Witches, while others said that the brothers themselves started the tales to keep people away (and to keep family close to home).

The married brother had a daughter, and he kept his family under such close watch they were nearly prisoners in their home. Years later, the daughter described her fear of the "earth babies," or six-foot humanlike beasts covered in red hair that came from the sand and howled like abandoned babies. Her father had also described a witch in the form of a cow; those who saw her as she flew by reportedly ended up dead. Then there was a serpent called Vivaron, some thirty feet long, which emerged at sunset.

Most such partnerships generally come to a bad end, a fact we know from the serial killer teams we study today. Thus, it's no surprise that these guarded paranoid men would eventually become suspicious of each other.

After selling a herd, the married brother returned to the ranch and told the single brother that he'd buried the gold he'd received in a ceramic pot. The bachelor wasn't happy. He demanded to know where it was. They got into a fight and the bachelor killed the married brother. The trouble was, now he *really* wouldn't find the location of that gold!

He believed that his sister-in-law must know where it was, so he threatened the woman and her daughter. Yet he let them have time to think about it. He left them alone overnight and they decided that facing Vivarion and the earth babies was less dangerous than dealing with the surviving member of Los Animales. They packed up and fled.

Since the single brother was now alone and vulnerable, a group of men formed a posse, went to the ranch, and hanged him for all the crimes he'd committed. The ranch buildings were boarded up and no one stuck around long enough to search for the remains of the many missing people.

Despite the verdant valley and availability of fresh water, the dark tales deterred most ranchers from selecting the area for their herds.

Then, in 1918, a descendant of the brothers, Juan Ignasio Archuleta, filed for a homestead patent. He acquired it but sold it two years later without ever living on the property.

The man who purchased it was a wealthy rancher, Miguel Gonzales. He knew of the ghost stories but a ranch hand assured Gonzales that the spooky tales didn't matter to him. It took just two weeks for this man to move off the property. His explanation: he could hear a man and woman arguing in the empty house. Gonzales sold the property to another rancher who then lost the deed in a card game.

Roy Pfaffle, the winner, gave the deed to his wife, Carol Bishop Stanley, and she registered it in her name in 1929. When they divorced years later, she kept the land. She moved into the one deteriorating home still standing and began to recreate the place as a guest ranch, which she called Ghost Ranch. She stayed there for seven years, and those who came after her rebuilt the place into a resort and educational retreat.

When Katherine visited, a few staff members said that there were sightings of ghosts, and one showed her a haunted bunkroom. They believe the ghost is a former ranch hand. It's not a murder story, though.

New York

Mass Disaster: Whose Fault?

The *New York Times* ran a chilling story on March 26, 1911. On the Saturday afternoon before, three upper floors of the Asch Building, a supposedly fireproof ten-story building on the corner of Greene Street and Washington Place, had caught fire. It spread rapidly, trapping many of the 600 employees of the crowded Triangle Waist factory (often called the Triangle Shirtwaist factory). Although employees from other businesses in the building had left hours before, the Triangle workers were still there, dutifully sewing tailored women's blouses, known as shirtwaists. It was around 4:40 P.M. In another five minutes, they would have been on their way out of the building. Some already had reached for their coats.

The fire started on the eighth floor, in a bin full of cloth scraps. It quickly spread to the hanging garments. Some workers managed to run to the stairs and escape, but flames soon blocked this route. Doors to one exit that swung inward were blocked when a panicked crowd pushed others up against them. Of the two freight elevators, one was out of service. This left just one possible exit for far too many people. Only fifteen could fit at once. When the elevator failed, people tried sliding down the cable, and a few killed others when they jumped into the shaft.

Nearly 100 people from the tenth floor made it onto the roof and escaped via neighboring buildings, where New York University students helped them. One student reported seeing grown men actually biting women and children to get access to an escape route. The lone fire escape soon collapsed from the weight of too many people.

Heat rose, making the rooms insufferable, so workers raced for the windows. Some stood looking down at the sidewalk 100 feet below.

Within minutes, fire alarms were ringing. But the fire companies were too far to help.

"Then one poor, little creature jumped," wrote the *Times* reporter. "There was a plate glass protection over part of the sidewalk, but she crashed through it, wrecking it and breaking her body into a thousand pieces. Then they all began to drop."

At first, people on the street who saw large objects flying at them thought someone inside was trying to save bolts of material. Then they realized that *women* were jumping. The observers screamed in horror and begged the women at the windows not to jump. They didn't realize what the employees on that floor who still clung to the window frames could see inside: people shrieking in agony as the fire consumed the materials around the shop and spread onto their clothes and hair.

"They jumped, they crashed through broken glass, they crushed themselves to death on the sidewalk." Sometimes two held hands. Six women managed to get to an electric cable. They all grabbed it together, and their weight proved to be too great. All fell to the street. Similarly, a human bridge to an adjacent building broke down from the weight of terrified escapees.

One girl waved a handkerchief at the crowd before leaping from a window adjoining the NYU Building on the west. Her dress caught on a wire, and the crowd watched her hang there till her dress burned free and she came toppling down to her death.

A young man stood on the narrow window ledge, offering his hand as, one by one, the women took it and allowed him to escort them to their doom before leaping himself with one of the women. She kissed him before they jumped together.

One fireman running ahead of a hose wagon, which was blocked by bodies, spread a net. Two others grabbed it. A girl, turning end over end, struck on the side of it. Everyone waited to see if she'd survived. She had, but others went right through the net. In one place, so many women crashed through a sidewalk that it created a five-by-five foot hole.

Five girls who stood close together at a window held their place while a fire ladder was raised toward them. But it stopped two stories short. They'd run out of time. Fire had caught them. Together, they leaped, clinging to one another, with fire streaming back from their hair. They struck a glass sidewalk cover and went through it into a basement.

In just half an hour, 146 people died, many of them just girls between 16 and 23. More than 50 had jumped or been pushed out. The people landing on top of them had crushed a few who might have survived. Many did not die on impact, but lingered in agony for a while. There were 71 people with nonfatal injuries.

Victims were laid out in wooden boxes on the sidewalk for sobbing relatives to try to identify, but many were burned or crushed beyond recognition. Sometimes, said the paper, it was a distinctive shoe or tooth that gave a decedent an identity. For a few, it was a piece of jewelry, a purse, or an engagement ring.

"A heap of corpses lay on the sidewalk for more than an hour," wrote a reporter. "The firemen were too busy dealing with the fire to pay any attention to people whom they supposed beyond their aid. When the excitement had subsided to such an extent that some of the firemen and policemen could pay attention to this mass of the supposedly dead they found about half way down in the pack a girl who was still breathing. She died two minutes after she was found."

Inside, 30 bodies blocked the elevator shaft, where girls had been trapped and were unable to move to a safer location. Another 50 or so were charred on the upper floors, and several were huddled in a cloakroom. Many bodies were placed in coffins right there on the street, while others were transported to the city morgue. Sadly, nearly three-dozen remained unidentified.

Triangle owners Isaac Harris and Max Blanck, known as the "Shirtwaist Kings," had been in the building as well, but had escape via the roof.

An investigation turned up the fact that the building had just one fire escape, which was hardly sufficient for the number of people in the building each and every day. However, the owners claimed they placed their trust in the fireproofing of the building. In fact, the building's exterior had survived mostly intact.

All who escaped recalled a flash of flames, leaping first among the girls in the southeast corner of the eighth floor and then suddenly over the entire room, spreading through the linens and cottons with which the girls were working.

What had burned so quickly were the shirtwaists, hanging on lines above tiers of workers, sewing machines placed too close for room to move between them, and shirtwaist trimmings and cuttings that littered floors.

The fire chief was outraged. He'd proposed better safety mechanisms for these buildings, but the Manufacturers' Association had blocked him. In fact, this building had experienced four recent fires and was considered unsafe due to the insufficiency of its exits. Charges of first- and second-degree manslaughter were soon filed against Harris and Blanck. There was talk that they routinely locked the fire escape to prevent thefts.

However, the building had violated no codes for those times and there was no evidence that the owners had known that the exit doors were locked. They were acquitted. This tragedy caused a ripple throughout the workers' unions and influenced dramatic changes in safety standards. In addition, Harris and Blanck lost a civil suit which forced them to pay the victims' families $75 each.

Just two years later, Blanck was fined for once again locking exit doors in his factory.

Despite the acquittals, it's clear that these businessmen created unsafe conditions and were responsible for this tremendous pain, suffering, and loss. No one was ever held accountable, and the owners actually profited from insurance payments.

The Asch Building is now the Brown Building.

The ghostly manifestations take the form of odors: smoke, and sometimes burning flesh. Sometimes locked doors are found unlocked. People who work in the building report seeing shapes drop past the window, but upon investigation, nothing is there.

Some people call this incident a tragic accident. We think that, despite the acquittal, it was more of a fine piece of lawyering that just saved it from being a crime scene. Technicalities aside, the poor decisions of two businessmen, aided by greedy organizations that crippled efforts to improve safety codes, directly contributed to these deaths in a criminal manner.

Staten Island Mansion

Creepy teenage horror movies often feature murders in haunted houses, but such is not often the case in real life. That's why a recent mob hit stands out from so many others. In 2005, 36-year-old Robert McKelvey was drowned in an ornamental pond on a Staten Island, New York estate known as Kreischer Mansion. He'd been stabbed and strangled, and after being drowned, his body was dismembered and burned in the furnace. But others have burned there as well.

Balthasar Kreischer built the Victorian mansion at Arthur Kill Road during the latter part of the nineteenth century, using proceeds from his prosperous brick and terra cotta factory. In fact, he'd built two mansions, one for his son and daughter-in-law, but that one had burned down, and the couple was consumed in the flames. There were rumors that Balthasar had recently been in a dispute with his son, so he came under suspicion. Still, the deaths were not classified as homicides. Apparently the surviving house retained the couple's spirits, because subsequent residents and others in the area reported the appearance of apparitions, unexplained banging, and slamming doors. This might have added some motive for luring McKelvey to the mansion.

Allegedly, McKelvey's death was a "hit" carried out by four reputed Bonanno crime associates. McKelvey, too, was a Bonanno associate and supposedly he'd failed to pay off a debt. In addition, he'd been talking too much about the gang's activities. It was surmised that groundskeeper Joseph Young had tricked McKelvey into coming, and the others had assisted with the murder and cover-up. The police got a tip, but when they went to find the furnace to process it for evidence, they learned that because the building was in the process of being remodeled as an assisted-living facility, the furnace had been replaced.

In an indictment unsealed in U.S. District Court in Brooklyn, investigators charged McKelvey's boss, Gino Galestro, and three others: Joseph Young, Stefan Cicale, and Jose Garcia. Galestro and Young were eligible for the death penalty. Galestro allegedly ordered the hit in April 2005, just before he pled guilty to a federal loan sharking charge. He had been sentenced to a year and one day in prison, as his associates recruited Young, with his convenient caretaking position, into the conspiracy with the promise of $8,000.

According to the indictment, Young was allegedly responsible for the hit, but he failed to strangle McKelvey, who broke free. Young ran after him and overcame him again, this time stabbing him repeatedly. Finally, he dragged the victim to the brick-lined pond and drowned him. The others then helped to cut up the body and dispose of it.

FBI agents searched the house for evidence, but did not reveal whether they encountered anything out of the ordinary.

North Carolina

Hamilton's Revenge?

Just past Kill-Devil-Hills at the Cape Hatteras National Seashore in North Carolina, is the largest sand dune on the Atlantic coast—Jockey's Ridge. By day, it's a Mecca for hang-gliders. Yet there was a time when it was a rather sinister place during the night.

It was Alexander Hamilton who instigated building the first lighthouse on the treacherous Cape Hatteras, and his action eventually spelled disaster to countless ships traveling further north that fell for an illusion. Early settlers in the area now known as Nag's Head included former pirates, who discovered a means to continue their theft without going to sea. They knew how easy it was for ships carrying wealthy cargo to lose direction, so they devised a trick to lure those ships onto the shoals. On a dark night, bands of cutthroats would affix a lantern to the neck of an old nag and lead it up on Jockey's Ridge. They then tied a weight to the horse's foot to make it limp, which resulted in forcing its head to bob up and down. The lantern then deceived commanders of targeted ships to alter their course. Once trapped on the shoals, the ships were easy pickings for the pirates, who boarded and murdered everyone. On starless nights, some folks say you can still hear the agonized shrieks of those tormented souls who died so mercilessly.

Jockey's Ridge State Park

There was one passenger, however, who'd been spared: Theodosia Burr, daughter of Aaron Burr, Hamilton's political enemy. Their intense animosity ended in a duel that killed Hamilton, considered an outright murder, and Burr was forced to hide out. He was indicted in New Jersey but never arrested. Eventually he moved to New York.

Theodosia had married a South Carolina politician. She had a son, who grew ill and died. Prostrate with grief, she decided to visit her father, so she boarded an ill-fated ship named *The Patriot.* When the pirates took the ship, they began to kill everyone. Theodosia's maid was tossed overboard before her eyes, and as one pirate was about to run Theodosia through with his sword, she lost her mind. Superstitious about insanity, the pirates took her to shore and left her in the care of local citizens.

No one knew who she was, although she carried a hand-painted portrait of herself—a gift for her father. She grew old and ill, and one day walked out into the ocean, leaving only tracks behind in the sand. Her portrait was given to a physician, who used it to discover her identity. The portrait is now in New York, but Theodosia remains on the Outer Banks. Along with the ghost crabs that skitter over the beach, she walks the sand when the sky is gray and the wind is high. She's most often seen by hardy residents who stay year-round between Christmas and New Year's.

It was an irony that, had Burr not shot him, Hamilton would have lived to finish installing proper lights along the coastline, preventing the sort of wreck that stole Burr's daughter from him. Burr himself haunts Wall Street (and possibly New Hope, Pennsylvania), while his last wife disturbs the air in New York's Morris-Jumel mansion.

Hatteras is also known for tales about Blackbeard's ghost. Edward Teach, a.k.a., Blackbeard the pirate, had been an intimidating man, nearly seven feet tall. His bushy black beard had covered his belt buckle. To make himself look like the devil, he'd worn firecrackers in his hair, along with a coil of smoking dried fungus as a cap.

Wild ponies still run free on Ocracoke Island, and it harbors small fishing villages, as it did in Blackbeard's day. He'd built his "castle" there (now razed), owned another house across the Pamlico Sound, and taken four wives in the surrounding area. When he decided to make Ocracoke his pirate's refuge, the governor of Virginia took action, sending a warship to raid the island and bring Blackbeard back. However, only the pirate knew how to navigate the shoals that protected his castle, and when the invading ship foundered, he boarded. He was shot and wounded in the head, yet he leapt onto the commanding officer with a howl. He encountered a sword thrust that nearly beheaded him, but remained on his feet. Blood spurting, he continued to fence with the officer, receiving more wounds until his beard was clotted with crimson. Then Blackbeard raised his pistol at his opponent, who backed away. His eyes clouded over and he fell down dead at the other man's feet. Thirty-seven wounds pierced his body.

His head was taken back to Virginia and the body tossed overboard. Legend has it that the headless corpse swam around the ship three times before sinking. Blackbeard's reported treasures were never located. However, some islanders claim that he walks the village of Ocracoke, looking for his head. Sometimes during the full moon, you can see his body near "Teach's Hole," gleaming in a phosphorescent light just beneath the water's surface. His ship, too, appears on the Pamlico Sound, portending doom.

Oklahoma

Unsolved Mystery

It was March 13, 1956, in Avard, Oklahoma, and 22-year-old Mildred Ann Reynolds, newly married and a senior at Northwestern Oklahoma State University, was killed and burned in her car.

Since she'd suffered from dizzy spells, some investigators dismissed her death as a tragic accident, but this notion failed to explain her blood-spattered shoe found more than 250 feet from the car, next to a patch of flattened grass, or her coat ten feet behind the car. In addition, there was an unusual burn pattern on the car, a bullet casing near it, and a set of tire tracks nearby that did not match Mildred Ann's car. To some, it looked like arson to cover a murder, so the case was presented to a coroner's jury.

The jury ruled Mildred's death a homicide. Nevertheless, there were no leads and the case went cold. However, from time to time, Mrs. Reynolds apparently still shows up. The owners of Vina Rae's Grill once described the day a woman dressed in green came in and sat down at a table. She made no eye contact and then simply vanished. The entrance bell did not chime for her entry or her exit.

They investigated and learned that Mildred Ann had worn green on the day she died and she'd resembled the woman who'd come in but placed no order.

Pennsylvania

Stunning Slaughter

According to the account in an 1881 pamphlet, "Murder of the Geogles and the Lynching of the Fiend Snyder," the incident occurred just after Christmas, on December 26. Jacob Geogle (also spelled Gogel in the Nazareth *Item*) and his wife, Annie, had a red house on the Monacacy Creek near the Santee Mill, about three miles north of Bethlehem. They had three girls, ages 11 to 14.

Jacob, 38, worked in the Coleman Iron Works and to help ends meet, had taken in a boarder, Edward Snyder. This man, age 24, was attracted to the eldest daughter, Alice, and on several occasions had tried to accost her. She told her parents, who warned Snyder to stay away from her. But Snyder was not a man to be ordered about. By all reports, he'd stop at nothing to get what he wanted.

The house was crowded on Christmas Day in 1880 as the Geogles entertained another couple, the Youngs (or the Fogels, depending on which account you read), with their two young daughters. The girls stayed over night.

After they all had settled in, Snyder quietly rose, lit a candle, and placed it in the kitchen, which was next to the Geogles' bedroom. He took an axe from the woodpile and opened the door. Jacob snored in his place closest to the wall. (One report describes them asleep on the floor). Snyder lifted the axe, bringing it down with such force that he cracked Jacob's skull. He repeated this with Annie. Then he proceeded to chop them up, spattering blood all over himself, the bed, the floor, and the walls. According to the pamphlet, "the mouths of both were cut nearly to the ears, and the necks were cut by repeated blows until the heads were nearly severed from the bodies." Snyder placed the axe across the bodies and went into the kitchen to remove his bloody shirt.

He then proceeded to the room where Alice and the Young's daughter were sleeping, intent on satisfying his lust. However, Alice was a strong girl and she screamed and fought him off. In the struggle, Snyder left behind bloody handprints, which would be evidence against him. One of the younger Geogles children ran to fetch her parents, but found their mutilated bodies instead. As she went back up the steps, Snyder seized the three younger girls and locked them in the bedroom with the two older girls before exiting the house.

He took refuge in the home nearby of an acquaintance named George Ritter, telling him that four burglars had entered the Geogles house and slaughtered them. Snyder claimed he'd fought with them, but they'd left through a window.

In the meantime, the children had broken out of the room, and men (perhaps called by Ritter) came to find the bodies. Snyder mingled among them, "cool" and indifferent, as they expressed horror over what they found and vowed vengeance on the murdering fiend. Apparently no one placed much stock in the tales told by children, because Alice pointed to the culprit and described his attempt to rape her. He managed to slip away.

George Ritter and George Young reported the incident to the local magistrate, who sent for the coroner and district attorney. Detective W. W. Yohe, who worked for the railroad, arrived as well.

As word spread, people started to come to the house to gaze at the gory mess. However, "few persons remained in the presence of the dead longer than an instant." Unbelievably, Snyder remained in the vicinity, mixing with people and repeating his absurd story about the quartet of burglars. Yet his calm demeanor raised suspicions.

Geogle House

Finally, two parties of five men each, armed with clubs and pitchforks, went looking for him. Yohe took charge and they soon came across Snyder hiding in the straw in Ritter's barn. As he jumped from the loft to the ground, some from the group yelled, "Hang him!" and "Cut his throat!"

Snyder was marched straight to Geogles' house, where the bodies still lay in bed, and subjected to an inquest. There, he admitted he'd done it. A number of people mentioned how much it would cost taxpayers to put him through a trial, and they recalled how Allen Laros, over in Easton, got a deal with an insanity ruling for poisoning his family. They worried that Snyder might get away with murder.

One man found a bed cord inside the home and brought it out to use, but Detective Yohe insisted on keeping Snyder alive for the DA. By now, the swelling crowd was calling for blood. They locked Yohe into the death chamber and dragged Snyder outside to a nearby chestnut tree.

While someone wrapped the cord around his neck, no one was willing to climb the tree and drape it over a branch. But Yohe, now free, stuck his hand between the cord and Snyder's neck, daring anyone to proceed.

Snyder continued to admit his deed, saying to Yohe, "I'm not afraid to die. I deserve to for what I have done. The old man and me had words some time ago and I said I would fix him and I always keep my word. I am glad I killed them, and would do the same thing over. I want to talk to you a minute and all I ask those devils is that they will wait until I get through."

But no one was about to give this killer any consideration. John Mack scrambled up the tree to place the rope over a limb. Snyder walked calmly over, ready. Yohe tried to save him, but "half a hundred willing hands" seized the rope and pulled, yanking Yohe off the ground three or four feet as Snyder rose into the air, choking. After five minutes, they let go of the rope, and Snyder fell with a thud back to the ground. He was unconscious. They re-hanged him, leaving him in place for three-quarters of an hour, and he finally died from strangulation. His body was removed and taken to the county poorhouse, although it's not clear where he was finally buried.

The DA wanted everyone directly involved to be arrested, but the local consensus was that no jury would convict anyone for this night's work. The prints of Snyder's bloody hands on the bed and sheets where he'd attacked Alice were sufficient evidence for his guilt, along with his confession.

Ghost stories soon grew up around the Geogles house and the chestnut tree. Some describe the victims and others indicate the Snyder roams about.

Murder in the Stacks

Further west in Pennsylvania, at Penn State University, Betsy Aardsma was murdered in the central stacks of the Pattee Library on November 28, 1969. She was a graduate student from Holland, Michigan, who was on campus over Thanksgiving break to do some research. She was found with a single stab wound to the heart, and two men were seen fleeing the library. One alerted the desk clerk that a girl "needed help" in the stacks.

Thousands of students and faculty were interviewed, but there were no substantial leads. No one could positively identify the men seen leaving the building, and the sparsely populated campus over Thanksgiving break provided very few witnesses. Within the past few years, articles have been published locally containing new information from private investigators, some of which have named viable suspects.

Reports from the library indicate that a female spirit haunts the stacks where Aardsma was murdered. Some people hear the ghostly echo of her final scream.

With fragmented leads gone cold, this would be an excellent case for PFI's to work on. Since it appears that Betsy Aardsma is probably the female ghost who haunts the library, paranormal investigators would attempt to get EVP directly from her, asking whether she knew her assailants, whether they were students or strangers to the University and if, indeed, there was more than one. Since a motive seems to be missing, that would be an important question to ask. If investigators could get permission, equipment could be set up overnight, such as a game-cam, in the stacks where she was murdered. A medium might also be used to attempt to remote view into the past to gain additional information.

The Wicked Innkeeper at Hawk Mountain

Thousands of people flock to Hawk Mountain during the migrational flights of hawks and eagles. Located off I-78, in the middle of Pennsylvania, the views overlook an amazing valley. The Hawk Mountain Bird Sanctuary provides educational exhibits and tours, but people can wander on the many paths (some easy, some difficult) to get to the best viewing locations for the winged raptors.

Hawk Mountain

The ground has long been sacred to Native American tribes like the Lenni-Lenape. Some say that native spirits still roam the area. Others claim it's the spirits of families slaughtered during Indian attacks.

One such homestead became a roadside inn during the 1860s. Margaret and Matthias Schambacher ran the place. But apparently, they did more than just offer a bed and breakfast. Reports spread that many of the Schambacher's guests disappeared. Some people whispered that the Schambachers would get their guests inebriated in order to murder them and steal their goods. The bodies were dismembered and tossed down a disused well. There were also rumors that they turned the meat into sausages.

Supposedly, Schambacher admitted his deeds on his deathbed, claiming over a dozen victims. He supposedly said that something that lived in the mountain had compelled him to do it. It was probably a paranoid hallucination, but to him, it seemed demonic. Schambacher died, and the legend says that when his body was lowered into the grave at the New Bethel Church Cemetery, a bolt of lightning struck his tombstone.

A man who took over the property was later found beheaded.

In 1938, someone donated the former inn to the Hawk Mountain Sanctuary. Employees began to report strange noises, such as footsteps and wails in the night that sound as if someone is being tortured. People who visit Schambacher's grave at night (and plenty do so during Halloween) claim to see circular balls of light, as well as figures that disappear.

The Botched Hanging

In the Delaware just off Easton's bank is Getter's Island, with an upstream tip that nearly touches Pennsylvania's bank. The small strip of land was named for Charles Goetter, or Götter, now often spelled Getter. A German immigrant, he was courting two women in 1833, Molly Hummer and Margaret Lawall, although he was in love only with Molly. When Margaret claimed she was pregnant, perhaps to force him to decide between them, Charles reluctantly married her but refused to live with her as man and wife. He'd apparently once said, "I'll have Molly Hummer if I have to walk on pins to get her."

Margaret worked as a maid on the estate of Peter Wagener and shortly after the wedding, when she was heavy with child, Charles came one night to take her for a walk. The next morning, her corpse was found in a quarry by Greenwood Avenue. Getter, the prime suspect, was arrested, but he refused to confess, so preparations commenced for a trial. Getter engaged the service of a famous and skillful lawyer, James Madison Porter, who helped to found Lafayette College. This alone made the proceedings sensational. With no witnesses to the incident, it appeared to be an easy case for this masterful attorney to win, but he had not counted on a young doctor who lived in the area and who had avidly studied the emerging forensic sciences.

During the nineteenth century, some American physicians had noticed that participating in a criminal case that garnered public interest could generate fame and advancement, just as celebrity trials do even today. In addition, these cases had proven a productive venue for demonstrating what the new medical science could do. Up to this point, only medicine and toxicology had made a forensic impact, and doctors in America looked to noted figures in France who had founded medico-legal programs in several prestigious universities. Dr. Samuel Gross, 28, had taken a course in medical jurisprudence at the Jefferson Medical School in Philadelphia. Unable to develop a practice there, he'd returned to his hometown, Easton. He thus ended up as a witness for the prosecution in the Getter case.

The trial commenced on August 19, 1833, lasting a week, and Gross took the stand. Having done a postmortem examination on the victim, he was certain Mrs. Getter had been strangled. Gross described the research to date from the advanced medico-legal professionals in France on signs of asphyxiation by strangulation and explained how he'd arrived at his own conclusions with this same science. Gross had experimented on animals, strangling and dissecting them to examine the signs of manual asphyxiation. He believed this would confirm his conclusions, but the medical experts for the defense said Margaret had died from apoplexy over stress from her strained relations with Getter. Thus, Getter was innocent.

Porter questioned Gross's approach and attacked him for failing to look at the victim's brain for a cause of death other than strangulation. Given the incomplete nature of his approach, Porter stated, how could he be so certain about his conclusions?

Undeterred, Gross stood by the new science. Porter brought in a dozen physicians to contradict young Gross, and they offered their diagnosis of apoplexy, but Dr. Gross stood his ground. Clearly, a good logical case could be made against Getter as well, and after only thirty-six minutes of deliberations, the jury found him guilty. He still protested his innocence, but a date was set for his hanging.

As the grim day approached, Getter confessed, affirming Dr. Gross's analysis.

Getter now had a date with the gallows. When the day arrived, Easton took on a carnival atmosphere, as tens of thousands of people from around the countryside poured in to see the event. Getter donned a white suit and was escorted into the streets by Sheriff Daniel Robb. A procession of people accompanied them along the half mile to the tiny island in the Delaware, where the gallows stood. At the shore, the killer, calm and collected, had to step across a series of boats strung together in a flotilla.

Getter had requested to be hanged by a method different from the typical drop-and-break approach: He wanted to be drawn up and choked. So the rope was placed around his neck and then drawn up fast. He struggled for a few minutes before the rope broke, throwing him to the ground.

"That was good for nothing," he said.

He had to wait, feeling the rope burn and contemplating his end for twenty-six minutes before a sturdier rope was found and brought to the island. To get on with it, he adjusted his scarf to hide the fresh mark on his neck. He then waited for the rope to tighten again. As Getter was lifted off his feet he struggled and kicked, and by some accounts, it took him fully eleven minutes to die. His body was left hanging for half an hour before it was removed for burial.

Getter's Island

People say that Getter's ghost walks around on the small island, perhaps due to the extra trauma he endured before dying.

His former wife is restless as well, it seems, and maybe she's unable to move on because she feels a little guilty. The tale came out afterward that she'd been a mother before, so Getter might not have been the man who had gotten her pregnant. In any event, they both died as a result.

The Boy in the Box

Katherine used to write for the Vidocq Society Newsletter, which is how she learned about the mystery surrounding the famous and tragic "Boy in the Box." Forensic artist Frank Bender (now deceased), along with Richard Walter and a retired U.S. Customs Special Agent,

Bill Fleischer, founded a special group of law enforcement personnel who meet each month in a posh restaurant in Philadelphia to brainstorm on long-unsolved cases. They called it the Vidocq Society, based on an ingenious French police spy from the eighteenth century.

Eugene Francois Vidocq had once been a criminal, and according to the story, he talked his way onto the police force by engineering an escape. He persuaded the Parisian police that because he was known to the criminal element as one of them, he could easily mingle and acquire information for arrests. He was so good at this that even those arrested didn't suspect him. Once they caught on, Vidocq continued his work in disguise. In 1811, he became the founder and first chief of the *Surete*, an elite undercover unit that rapidly gained international fame. Having influenced the development of many fictional characters, he's considered the father of modern criminal investigation.

The Vidocq Society has grown to a membership of several hundred. They even adopted the "Boy in the Box" case as their own. The case had haunted the patrolman who first came across the body, and when he joined the Society years later, he brought the case with him.

On February 25, 1957, on the outskirts of northeastern Philadelphia near Fox Chase, a young man following a rabbit into a weedy lot found a body wrapped in a flannel blanket inside a cardboard box. Investigators estimated the blonde Caucasian boy to have been between the ages of 4 and 6. He was malnourished and had been badly beaten. Even so, someone had recently trimmed his nails and hair, and hair clippings clung to his body. With the time of death uncertain, the cause was determined to be severe head trauma from multiple blows.

The box had held a bassinet purchased locally, a man's customized cap was found near the scene and traced to the seller, and the boy's nude body had been wrapped in two sections of a distinctive blanket. He had seven scars from medical treatment and eight moles. He might also have had an eye ailment.

Yet every potential lead dried up. Days turned into months, and months into years without a resolution.

Some investigators continued to search on their own time and at their own expense. In 1998, the Vidocq Society adopted the case. They rechristened the boy America's Unknown Child. Sam Weinstein, an officer who was present at the initial crime scene, led their re-investigation. Later former investigators Joseph McGillen and William Kelly took over. The boy's remains were exhumed for DNA testing and then reinterred in a better location in Ivy Hill Cemetery at Easton Road.

America's Most Wanted aired a segment about the case, which inspired George Knowles, a private citizen, to get involved. When he was eleven, he'd seen a flyer about the crime at a local police station. He watched the airing and then joined an Internet discussion group whose postings were monitored by the Vidocq Society.

Word got around. In June 2002, Kelly, McGillen, and a Philadelphia homicide detective interviewed a woman who had offered information through her psychiatrist. She described an abusive mother, a librarian, who had purchased a toddler in the mid-1950s whom they called Jonathan. Her parents had kept him in a box in the cellar, and her mother killed him when she banged his head on the bathroom floor after he vomited one day and made a mess. The woman recalled the blanket in which they had wrapped him and the box into which they had placed him. She herself had trimmed his fingernails, while her mother cut his hair. Her initial disclosures, the psychiatrist attested, had predated the AMW broadcast and the website.

The details were accurate, yet while neighbors from her former residence remembered her, which confirmed some of the woman's story, no one recalled the boy. Since the tale is based only on memories, Philadelphia police will not close the case.

Bender created a male bust that he believed would resemble the boy's father. It was published in several places in the hope that someone would know a person with similar features who once had a son.

On the Internet, someone posted a ghost story attached to this case. Supposedly, if one goes after dark to the place where he was found, his ghost can be seen walking around. One night, some boys obsessed with the tale decided to camp out and watch. The boys were just getting into their tents to bed down when they heard a moaning noise. One boy ventured out and claimed to have seen a figure that he first thought was an animal. Then he recognized the boy from the various sketches made for newspapers. He tried to speak to this figure, but it just vanished in front of him.

South Dakota

Deadwood

On August 2, 1876, according to the *Black Hills Pioneer*, Jack McCall strode toward James Butler "Wild Bill" Hickok as he played a hand of poker. It was just after 4:00 P.M. on a hot afternoon in Deadwood, South Dakota. Saloon #10 was a hangout for card players, but McCall had another agenda. Coming up behind Hickok on the only day that Wild Bill had ever sat with his back to the door, he raised his .45 single-action revolver and shot him in the back of the head. "Damn you, take that!" he shouted.

Hickok fell from his chair and hit the floor.

Born in Illinois in 1837, Hickok had gained notoriety as a gunfighter in 1861, when he shot three men in self-defense. News articles, dime novels, and comic books enhanced his fame, especially as he continued to get into gunfights that he survived. (Reportedly, he killed 36 men.) He became a Texas lawman, but accidentally shot his deputy. He was removed from his post. Subsequently, he avoided gunfights. He made his living in Buffalo Bill Cody's Wild West Show before turning to a life of gambling. In 1876, he went to

Deadwood and became a regular at the poker tables of the #10 Saloon.

The city of Deadwood had been founded in the early 1870s, on land that had been granted to the Lakota tribe in the 1868 Treaty of Laramie. Thus, its existence was illegal. In 1874, General Custer launched a gold rush there, and Deadwood soon became a lawless town, with a population of about 5,000.

Deadwood Today
Photo Courtesy of Ingrid Pochron

So, on August 2, after shooting Hickok, McCall tried to shoot others, but reportedly his remaining cartridges were duds. He ran from the saloon and tried stealing a horse, but he fell off. McCall ran into a local butcher shop and tried to hide, but he was located and arrested.

Those who rushed to the saloon after hearing the gunshot found Hickok senseless on the floor, blood gushing from his wound. The exit wound had torn out his right cheek. An autopsy showed that the bullet had gone straight through the base of the brain and had loosened several molars as it passed through. Part of the brain squeezed out through the facial wound. It took the coroner's jury no time to decide that McCall should be tried for murder.

According to legend, when he died, Hickok had a pair of black aces and black eights, a combination that has since been known as the Dead Man's Hand. (Whether there was a fifth card, as is typical of a poker hand, is unknown.)

That evening, officials were elected to conduct the trial. It would be a speedy proceeding, taking place the very next morning.

At the appointed hour, Sheriff Joseph Brown led McCall into the theater and placed him into a chair on the stage, next to Judge Kuykendall. To select jurors, a hundred names were placed into a hat and pulled out one by one until an appropriate jury was seated.

"Order in the court," said the judge. He asked the people present to sustain him in his unpleasant duty.

A newspaper article printed the following about the defendant: "Never did a more forbidding countenance face a court than that of Jack McCall. His head, which is covered by a thick crop of chestnut hair, is very narrow as to the parts occupied by the intellectual portion of the brain, while the animal development is exceedingly large. A small sandy mustache covers a sensual mouth. The nose is what is commonly called 'snub,' cross eyes, and a florid complexion, and the picture is finished. He was clad in a blue flannel shirt, brown overalls, heavy shoes; and as he sat in a stooping position with his arms across his breast, he evidently assumed a nonchalance and bravado which was foreign to his feelings, and betrayed himself by the spasmodic heavings of his heart."

There were plenty of eyewitnesses to the deed, and those who'd been in the game gave testimony about what they saw. It was clear that McCall's intent, from the way he walked into the room and deliberately shot Wild Bill, had been premeditated. Nothing had provoked him in the heat of the moment. This was a case of cold-blooded murder.

A few character witnesses defended McCall, describing him as anything but quarrelsome. Some witnesses called for the defense gave the decedent a bit of a bashing, saying that as a "shootist," he'd terrorized towns wherever he went. Quick on the draw, he'd killed many men.

When McCall spoke on his own behalf, he said, "Well, men, I have but few words to say. Wild Bill killed my brother, and I killed him. Wild Bill threatened to kill me if I ever crossed his path. I am not sorry for what I have done. I would do the same thing over again."

The prosecution then asked for clarity from several people who'd known Hickok. The upshot, according to the *Black Hills Pioneer*, was that "he had never imposed on anyone, and that in every instance where he had slain men, he had done so either in the discharge of his duty as an officer of the law or in self defense."

The jury dispatched its duty quickly. Soon after the two-hour trial, the verdict was "not guilty." Hickok's associates (and the newspaper editor) believed that Wild Bill had been cheated of justice.

Hickok's body was placed on some boards and carried across the creek to Hickok's friend, Colorado Charlie. He sent out a notice: "Funeral notice. Died, in Deadwood, Black Hills, August 2, 1876, from the effect of a pistol shot, J. B. Hickok (Wild Bill), formerly of Cheyenne, Wyoming. Funeral services will be held at Charley Utter's camp, on Thursday afternoon, August 3, 1876, at 3 o'clock. All are respectfully invited to attend."

Those who came got a viewing of Wild Bill in a silver-ornamented coffin. "His long chestnut hair, evenly parted over his marble brow," said the *Pioneer*, "hung in waving ringlets over the broad shoulders. His face was cleanly shaved excepting the drooping mustache, which shaded a mouth—which in death almost seemed to smile, but which in life was unusually grave. The arms were folded over the stilled breast, which enclosed a heart that had beat with regular pulsation amid the most startling scenes of blood and violence. The corpse was clad in a complete dress suit of black broadcloth, new underclothing, and a white linen shirt. Beside him in the coffin lay his trusty rifle, which the deceased prized above all other things, and which was to be buried with him in compliance with an often expressed desire."

Someone had dug a grave on the mountainside. A procession accompanied the closed coffin to this site. On a large stump at the head of the grave, the following inscription was cut: "A brave man—the victim of an assassin—J. B. Hickok (Wild Bill), aged 48 years; murdered by Jack McCall, August 2, 1876."

About six weeks later, U. S. authorities arrested McCall in Laramie City, Wyoming. He'd bragged a little too loudly that he'd killed Wild Bill Hickok in a gunfight. Wyoming officials ignored the acquittal, since Deadwood was not a legally recognized jurisdiction. The federal court covering Dakota Territory agreed and set a date for a retrial.

McCall admitted that Wild Bill had never killed his brother. Instead, his motive had been revenge over Hickok taking a card from him during a poker game. Later, he said that John Varnes had hired him to kill Hickok over a nasty dispute in Denver. McCall was willing to give up Varnes to get a deal for himself.

It didn't work out. He was convicted in January 1877, and sentenced to be hanged. This was carried out on March 1, 1877. McCall, the first person to be executed by federal officials in Dakota territory, was just 24 years old. The noose was left around his neck when he was buried.

Another version of the tale turned up in a Wyoming newspaper. In this one, McCall was in a poker game with

Hickok the day before the shooting. He bet more than he had and lost, then found himself short of money to pay up. Hickok chastised him for poor planning but gave him $5 to cover food and lodging. McCall apparently felt humiliated and in revenge, shot his benefactor.

Wild Bill's remains were exhumed and transferred to Mount Moriah Cemetery. Charlie Utter also purchased this lot. "There was no odor or no perceptible decay, and it is supposed by those who examined it that petrifaction had taken place, as it was hard as wood and returned the same sound as a log when struck with a stick.... His hair was as glossy and silky as when in life.... His mustache was as hard and seemed like his body to have been petrified." They estimated his weight at nearly 500 pounds.

In Deadwood today, the killing of Hickok and capture of McCall is reenacted for tourists every evening during the summer. You can also see Wild Bill's supposed "death chair."

But what about the paranormal?

Reportedly, Hickok had told Charlie Utter that he believed that Deadwood would be his final camp. He also wrote a note to his wife that suggested they might never meet again. Although he never sat with his back to the door, he did on the day of his assassination.

Some say that Hickok's restless soul still wanders the place, in the original saloon (which has burned down and been rebuilt several times, and is not the *current* Saloon #10). Some of the arcade games apparently play by themselves.

Others say that Deadwood's primary ghost is that of Seth Bullock, a longtime resident of Deadwood who built a hotel there in 1895. Bullock is the star of HBO's 2004–06 series, *Deadwood*, although Wild Bill is a character during the first season.

The Bullock Hotel is at 633 Main Street. Seth arrived in Deadwood the day before Hickok was murdered. Because he'd been in law enforcement previously, he subsequently became sheriff. At the hotel, guests report being tapped on the shoulder when no one is there, being pushed on the stairs, having things moved in their rooms, and seeing apparitions. One is Bullock himself and another is a little girl in Old West garb.

Texas

University of Texas Shooter

The clock tower on the campus of the University of Texas at Austin stands over three hundred feet high. From its observation deck is a 360-degree view of the campus and city. It was from this spot Charles Whitman, a 25-year-old troubled student, decided to shoot people at random on August 1, 1966. He ushered in the age of mass murder in America.

It was nearly 11:30 A.M. when Whitman came onto the campus, using the pretense of delivering something to a professor. This gave him a parking space close to the University of Texas administration building. In his car was a footlocker full of supplies and survival gear, and in the trunk a virtual arsenal: rifles, shotguns, a carbine, two pistols, a revolver, and ammunition.

He used a wheeled dolly to haul his heavy load into a service elevator. From the 27th floor he hauled his trunk and weaponry up to the observation deck on the 30th floor. He ran into a female greeter and hit her with the butt of a shotgun. Then he shot her and hid her unconscious body.

Whitman blocked the door to the stairs, but then two boys tried to get in. He fired at them with a spray of pellets. Two people died and two others were critically wounded. Whitman went to the observation deck, wedged his dolly against the door, and prepared for his ultimate event. He stood under the gilt-edged clock's south face, looking around.

Classes had let out and many students were walking across the paved campus mall. Whitman watched them, but it was too late for him to take full advantage. The delay caused by running into those people had cost him. There were fewer people walking across the green than he'd expected. He proceeded with the plan. At 11:48, Whitman lifted the scoped 6-mm Remington, aimed, and pulled the trigger. Once, twice, again and again. People began to fall to the ground, dead or wounded.

Police officers converged on the campus, coming in waves, joined by residents with their private weapons.

People shot up at the tower, hitting the clock face, but Whitman was well protected.

Three officers and a civilian ran into the building and up the stairs to storm the tower. Alerted to the madman's location, they went out to the deck. The officers jumped forward and surrounded a blond man on the deck, who had a radio tuned to the news. He turned and aimed at them, but they got him first. To make sure, they shot him six times.

It was 1:24 P.M. Fourteen people lay dead, and thirty-two were critically wounded. Investigators soon learned that on the night before his rampage, Whitman had killed his wife and mother.

As early as 1981, the "Old Main" tower was believed to be cursed, in part because its bricks had come from a haunted creek. Since Whitman's rampage, there have been several suicides and an accidental fall. The tower was finally closed to public tours. Supposedly, the ghosts of the suicide victims, and sometimes Whitman himself are reported in or near the tower. Flickering lights have spooked the security guards.

Murder Mansion

Nir Golan had just purchased a home in Seabrook, Texas, near Houston. In April 2014, he was preparing to move in when he discovered a disquieting fact. It was the scene of a rather high-profile murder. It was also reputed to be haunted.

During the early 1980s, Bill List was a successful entrepreneur, making trailers to haul drilling pipes. Few who knew him in Texas realized that he'd served time in Ohio for sexual offenses. His prey was adolescent boys. He would hire them to work around his house and then lure them inside. His specialty was sadomasochistic torture.

With his newfound wealth, List built a 34,000-square-foot mansion, complete with an indoor swimming pool, Jacuzzi, and a fountain. It also had bars. List would cruise around looking for young male street hustlers, which he kept captive in his mansion. One day in 1984, four of those young men turned on him and killed him. They stole money, credit cards and checks, jumped into List's car, and went on a spending spree. Using a forged check did them in, and they were arrested.

Bizarrely enough, in 1983, List's daughter had been the victim of infamous pickaxe killer, Karla Faye Tucker, who has since been executed.

The house, which most people considered hideous and cheaply gaudy, was put up for sale. However, it sat for a very long time without a single buyer showing interest. There were a few renters, but no one stayed long. Finally, a land developer tore it down and built condos on the land.

Residents in these condos have reported strange sightings, sounds, and impressions that have given the area the reputation of being haunted. Supposedly, people have seen the shadows of children on the grounds.

This, of course, is an example of a residual haunting. Often people can't figure out why their house is haunted when they are the first owners and they know it is new construction with no history of death or violence. They don't realize that if human emotional energies can be imprinted upon inanimate objects such as houses, they certainly can be imprinted on the very earth upon which these structures are built.

This leads to one of the more interesting theories as to why ghosts seem "trapped" in certain areas. It was first brought to Mark's attention by Joe Farrell, a paranormal researcher who came to Gettysburg with Cecil Downing, one of Pennsylvania's premier dowsers. Joe's thought was that the indigenous quartz-infused granite that is all over the battlefield could have absorbed the energy thrown off by the soldiers in combat. Mark was intrigued.

"I started doing research on capacitors, which are made of natural materials and store electricity. Then I realized that quartz is also affected by electricity, as in quartz watches. Research into the geology of the Gettysburg battlefield confirmed that the igneous intrusions of granite are indeed quartz-filled. The houses in Gettysburg are built on granite, fieldstone foundations and the salmon-colored brick used in the pre-battle houses is local; in other words, the clay was dug from the very fields infused with quartz. Then it occurred to me: quartz—silicon—is the material that stores electrons in a specific order in our computers. Now, how could humans imprint their images on the natural quartz?

"I knew that humans are 'electric beings.' It's why electro-cardiogram machines work. Also, there was that groundbreaking book by Dr. Robert O. Becker, *The Body Electric*, which details all the electric producing, or consuming parts of the body—muscles, brain, heart and so forth.

"I found that a Polish scientist, Janusz Slawinski, while researching the Shroud of Turin discovered that human beings, at the moment of death, give off up to a thousand times more photons than while alive. He called it a 'light shout.' I also read that human bones, being porous, give off piezoelectricity when broken. With the large number of casualties in battles, bullets broke thousands of bones and the surgeon sawed through thousands during treatment for wounds. The bursts of electricity were numerous throughout the days of battle and surgery.

"So the bursts of electricity given off by the dead, dying and wounded, imprinted themselves upon the quartz in the area, and, by some means we are still not certain of, are released in a form recognizable by the living as sounds and sights.

"Of course, the great question is, how is the energy released? If we can determine that, we can recreate the ghostly happenings anytime we want."

Virginia

Spirits of all Varieties

The Winery at La Grange was formally launched in December 2005, in Prince William County, Virginia. Paranormal activity drew the Nesbitt team there, and in the process, the team psychic turned up an undocumented murder.

The Winery at La Grange

Research into La Grange's past has revealed interesting folklore. One story in particular is about a piano playing in the (formerly) abandoned and vacant house. In early

2006, a family of four walked over to see the changes being made to the building. The house was locked and the mother and father walked around back while their two children tried to enter through the front door. As the parents shook a backdoor lock they heard piano music playing inside. Being a musical family, they listened and one of the parents said, "The children must have opened the front door and found a piano." They found an unlocked side door and called out to the children. The music stopped. The parents soon discovered that their kids were still outside, and *they* thought their parents had been playing the piano. The winery owners subsequently discovered that during the nineteenth century, owner Benoni Harrison had willed to his nephew "the piano in the parlor."

There are also recurring reports of the ghost of a young girl who inhabits one of the upstairs rooms. There is no story of a murder, but our psychic, Laine, sensed a strong male presence in a second floor room. She stated that his name was Daniel Jessup and he had lived there during the early 1900s. He said little to her, but she discovered that he had gotten into an argument with his brother-in-law over land that his deceased wife had owned. The fight escalated into violence. Daniel stabbed the other man, who shot and killed him. He bled out onto the wooden floorboards.

We could all see dark stains on the boards in this room, which could have been blood that was never properly removed. We mentioned this to the owners, in case they wanted to have this checked.

An investigation would involve going through records to see if such a person had ever lived there, and it could also include having a criminalist use current forensic methods to test the stains for the presence of blood. This would be an example of trying to document something a psychic envisioned. A name match would be unimpressive, since the place could have been researched prior to arriving, but the presence of blood soaked into boards would be rather sensational.

An attempt to look for records turned up nothing for this time period and name.

Church Going Spirits

From Fredericksburg comes the story of Aquia Church, one of the more haunted sites in the area. The original Aquia Church burned in 1751. The second and current church was built in 1757. Sometime during the American Revolution, a murder was committed on the very floor under which early parishioners lie awaiting the final resurrection. For almost two hundred years, until it was covered over by reinforcing cement, one of the flagstones in the floor of the center aisle of the church was stained with the blood of the young woman who was killed in the sanctuary. The murdered woman's body was then hidden in the belfry. The church had been abandoned for a number of years after that, so the body went undetected until, when it was finally discovered, there was nothing left but a skeleton with long blonde hair still attached to a grinning skull.

For decades it has been rumored that not even the bravest of Stafford County have been able to force themselves to enter Aquia Church near midnight, for it is then that the sounds begin.

The noises are so loud, so distinct, that they can be heard by those brave enough to merely walk past the church at night. Reports claim that from within can be heard "heavy noises" indicative of a struggle; as well, there are the sounds of feet running up, then down the stairs to the belfry. If the passerby is brave enough to enter the church, all sounds immediately cease.

Aquia Church

Sometime prior to the 1930s, a woman who was interested in the supernatural determined that she would document any evidence that Aquia Church was haunted. Since midnight was supposed to be the hour at which paranormal activities allegedly began, that is when she would conduct her investigation. But, try as she might, she could get no one in Stafford County to accompany her. She finally recruited two investigators from Washington, D.C., who were experts in audio so that they may record any anomalies that were reputed to happen within the church. They arrived just before midnight, and the woman was soon to discover that there were more than mere auditory apparitions present in Aquia Church. As soon as she set foot in the church a hand slapped her hard in the face. Hearing the hard blow and her scream, the other investigators rushed past her, but could find no one else in the church. With the addition of violence, the investigation suddenly ended. For days afterward, the red mark of the phantom hand remained upon her face.

Earlier in the twentieth century there were persistent reports of the sighting of a young woman, with long blonde hair, periodically peering out through the windows of the church. Fed up with what he thought were silly superstitions, one of the men in the neighborhood decided he would prove to the others that there was nothing to be frightened of. He said he would climb to the belfry that night. They teased him and said that he would probably just go into the doorway, wait a minute or two, then emerge, merely claiming he had visited the dreaded belfry. He would show them. He took a hammer and a nail out of his truck and into the church; he would climb to the belfry and hammer the nail into the wood there as evidence he had visited; they could check his work the next morning...or whenever they gathered enough courage.

He entered the church and his friends waited outside, laughing nervously. Ten minutes passed. Then twenty. They began to call softly to him. Was he all right? Come on, now, he could come out. The joke's over.

Forty minutes pass, and his friends are beginning to worry. Did he fall and hurt himself? Is he inside that awful place, unconscious, bleeding perhaps? His friends summoned their courage. A good hour had passed by the time they got some lanterns, and still nothing from their friend. They were shocked when they finally reached the belfry. There was their friend, hammer lying next to him, his eyes frozen open, his mouth contorted in a silent scream. In the dark he had hammered the nail through his own coat and into the belfry. When he tried to leave, it must have felt as if something had grabbed him and held him fast. Believing it was whatever evil resides within the church that had imprisoned him and refused to let him go, his heart gave out and he died of fright.

What is known in paranormal circles as a "harbinger" occurred during the Civil War. William Fitzhugh from Fredericksburg was a Confederate soldier. He and a fellow soldier had been scouting the area of Aquia. It was night, they were exhausted, and decided to spend the night, in spite of its reputation of being haunted, in the antiquated church. They decided they would leave the door open so they might hear any activity outside.

Curled up in the pews, they began what would be a restless night. Sometime after midnight, they were both awakened by the shuffling of feet on the flagstones at the rear of the church. Both were immediately awake, but hidden by the pews. Could it be a Yankee? Then, the whistling began. Eventually, they recognized the ancient tune: *The Campbells are Coming.* It stopped. The steps were even closer, halfway up the aisle, and the whistling started again. The two young men looked at each other in the dark, afraid to peep over the pew. The whistling stopped. Again, this time, right next to them, came the footsteps. And finally, again the whistling. Together they leapt from the pew and struck a match to find...nothing before them. But, from the road in front of the church they heard the unmistakable sound of Yankee cavalrymen. Fully awake, thanks to the frightening footsteps and ghostly whistling, they crawled out the back windows of the church, found their horses, and rode off, convinced they had been saved by the timely appearance of a ghost.

Aquia Church could be the scene of an investigation to determine if the young woman knew her assailant. EVP could produce some names—of both victim and perpetrator—which can then be checked against historical records. No doubt her disappearance, as well as the discovery of her remains, would have been recorded somewhere. Perhaps just this kernel of a clue could lead to the identification of a murder victim and perhaps her murderer. Or, it could lead to a complete debunking of a centuries-old ghost story.

Mistress of Murder

Belle Grove Plantation is located near Middletown, south of Winchester, Virginia. Thomas Jefferson had a part in designing the over-100-foot-long mansion, completed in 1797. Isaac Hite, Jr., the grandson of one of the earliest settlers in the Shennandoah Valley, after attending William and Mary College, served in the Continental Army attaining the rank of Major. In 1783, he married Nelly Conway Madison, sister of the future president James Madison who visited the plantation several times, even spending part of his honeymoon there. After his first wife's death, the Major married Ann Tunstall Maury, with whom he added ten more children to the three from his first marriage. Amazingly for the time period, all but one survived to adulthood. Major Hite continued to add to his holdings and the plantation eventually consisted of slave quarters, a large stone smokehouse with a fine flagstone path to it, and an icehouse. Hite also owned a general store, distillery, gristmill and sawmill. Belle Grove was sold out of the Hite family upon his and Ann's deaths.

As the Civil War loomed, one Benjamin Coolie (or Cooley) was living at Belle Grove with a handful of servants. His cook and housekeeper was a fiery young woman named Harriette Robinson. As a house servant, she enjoyed a softer lifestyle than the field hands. Whether there was something more going on between Harriette and the bachelor Benjamin is a matter of speculation, but Marguerite du Pont Lee, in her classic 1930 book, *Virginia Ghosts*, wrote that Harriett was heard to say that if a mistress were to ever enter the house she would not live long.

Eventually, Coolie did take a wife. Harriette was blatant in her disregard for the new Mrs. Coolie's authority. According to L. B. Taylor in *Haunted Virginia* (Stackpole Books), the hostility was so bad that the wife asked her husband to get rid of Harriette. Perhaps tellingly, he didn't.

The contretemps eventually erupted into physical altercations, with Mrs. Coolie beating Harriette with a broomstick over a missing stocking. Soon after, Mrs. Coolie was giving orders to Harriette in the basement of the house and ended up with her skull split with an ax, her body dragged down the flagstone path and thrown into the smokehouse. Harriette was seen leaving the smokehouse by some of the other slaves and later arrested.

Those who found Mrs. Coolie were astounded at the savagery of the attack, which apparently continued in the smokehouse: her right cheekbone was broken; two deep gashes on her forehead went down to the bone; knuckle marks were all about her face; fingernail scratches on her throat indicated she had been choked; when found, her feet were in the smokehouse fire burning. Yet she was still alive.

When she regained consciousness, she claimed that she had merely fallen. For some reason, perhaps a threat upon her husband, she refused to implicate Harriette. But her injuries were so severe that a fall could not have been the cause. She died a few days later without shedding any more light.

According to Taylor, circumstantial evidence against Harriette was overwhelming: the threats upon Mrs. Coolie's life, previous altercations, a dress Harriette washed right after Mrs. Coolie's beating, and the testimony from another slave that Harriette had asked her for poison and stated that she didn't care if they caught her and hanged her, that she would "have my revenge!"

Tried, convicted and sentenced, with no sign of remorse, she still beat the hangman.

L. B. Taylor has documented that she died in prison while awaiting execution. Marguerite du Pont Lee wrote that while she was incarcerated, the Yankees rolled through that section of Virginia and released all black prisoners from the jail. Harriette Robinson disappeared. "Ever since," wrote du Pont Lee, "the ghost of Mrs. Coolie has walked."

In *Virginia Ghosts* she wrote that within twenty years of Mrs. Coolie's horrible death, several members of the Rose family, who occupied the house, saw the same ghost often. They described a white figure standing by the fireplace in the basement. They would see it floating down the flagstone path—the same one Mrs. Coolie was dragged down—to the smokehouse. Again the white wraith would appear in the hallway of the mansion, or peer from the windows.

The current owners are more prone to emphasize the impressive history of the plantation, rather than its ghosts, but from one of the tour guides come a couple stories, not necessarily tied to Henrietta's crime. Visitors to Belle Grove have seen a woman in black in one of the upper windows. Considering the plantation's close vicinity to the 1864 battlefield of Cedar Creek, a remnant visitor in mourning would not surprise anyone.

And there was the UPS man who drove up to deliver a package. He knocked on the door and a little girl with lovely golden curls answered and let him in, after which she bounded up the stairs. Just then the resident entered the house from a shopping trip and asked the UPS man how he had gotten in since she had locked the door when she left. He said that the woman's little daughter let him in, to which the woman replied that she had no daughter. The UPS man left hurriedly, and the woman searched in vain for the little intruder. Some have speculated that it was the ghost of the one child of Major and Mrs. Hite who died before she had a chance to grow up.

Victims

Colorado

Featured on "Haunting Evidence" and the subject of many independent paranormal investigations is the spacious house at 755 15th Street in Boulder, CO, where JonBenét Ramsey was murdered. One investigator said he felt a "thick sadness" about the house and another claimed she couldn't breathe as she approached it. Someone posted on an online site that her mother had seen JonBenét's ghost on the day the girl had died; yet a psychic claimed that the child's ghost does not haunt the house. Another one says the child speaks to her and has told her who killed her (but no arrests have been made). Given how much publicity there has been, it's difficult to know how much the psychics have been influenced.

Ramsey House

So, let's look at the forensics. Katherine once worked with former FBI profiler Gregg McCrary on a profile of this case for Court TV, and we summarize McCrary's findings below.

With such incidents, we consider the time of day it occurred, the type of crime it was, the type of weapon used, whether it was high risk for the victim or high risk for the perpetrator, how it was accomplished, and whether there was evidence of mental illness or fantasy rituals. In addition, the offender might have left trace evidence behind or taken items away, any of which can help us to judge his or her comfort level with that type of crime, and his or her degree of criminal sophistication. We can take an educated guess about the motivation, the offender's experience with other types of crimes, and his or her possible level of education and type of work, as well as age and race.

It was December 26, 1996, at 5:52 A.M., when Patricia "Patsy" Ramsey, called 911 to say that her 5-year-old daughter had been kidnapped. The Boulder police sent an officer. He noted that Patsy was upset, although her husband, John, seemed calmer and more in control. They had another child in the home, 9-year-old Burke, who was still in bed.

Patsy said she had gone into JonBenét's second-floor bedroom to prepare her for a trip and found her bed empty. Patsy went down a back staircase to the first floor, and on a lower step she found a three-page note, written in black felt-tip pen on white, lined legal paper and laid out with the pages alongside one another. Directed to her husband, "Mr. Ramsey," the author demanded certain conditions, including that he not call the police and that he prepare to pay $118,000.

A crime-scene evidence team was called in and a trace put on the phone line. There were no signs of forced entry, although one friend, Fleet White, went on his own into the basement and did a cursory inspection; he noticed a broken window. John Ramsey admitted breaking it a few months before when he'd forgotten his key.

From the moment the police arrived, the crime scene was compromised because the house was not secured. The note had been moved and the Ramsey friends had been allowed to walk around freely. The deadline for the kidnappers' call came and went without any communication.

By noon, most of the official personnel had left, except for Detective Linda Arndt, but seven civilians were in the home. Arndt directed John Ramsey to search the house, and to take a friend with him. At 1:00 PM, he and Fleet White started in the basement. Around 1:20, Ramsey opened the door of a dark room and discovered his daughter's body on the floor. She lay on her back, her arms over her head bound with a cord, another cord wrapped around her neck, and her torso wrapped in a white blanket. A piece of black duct tape was over her mouth. Although she was dressed, close by lay her favorite pink nightgown.

John Ramsey ripped off the duct tape, removed the blanket, and tried to take off the binding. Then he carried the body upstairs. The child was laid out and covered with a blanket. Because of the holiday, the coroner, Dr. John Meyer, was delayed. At 8:00 P.M., he moved the body to the morgue.

During the autopsy, Meyer found chunks of pineapple in JonBenét's upper digestive tract. He removed a ligature from her neck and right wrist. An abrasion was on her right cheek, and another on the left side of her neck, and others on the right shoulder and left lower leg. A ligature bruise was on her right wrist. There were also dotted pattern injuries to her cheek and torso. A spot of blood was inside her panties and around her vagina, there were petechial hemorrhages on her eyelids, lungs, and neck. In addition, there was a large hemorrhage on the right side of her skull, over an eight-inch fracture and a bruising of the brain. The cause of death was determined to be asphyxiation by strangulation, and there had been trauma to the vaginal tissues. She'd also suffered blunt force trauma to the head, after strangulation.

Physical evidence and potential evidence in this cases consisted of:

- The ransom note and practice note
- A bowl of pineapple in the kitchen with Patsy's and Burke's fingerprints
- Two tablets of lined white paper from in the house, with a page of "practice" writing
- Sharpie pens that proved to have been used in the writing of the note and practice note, placed back where they belonged in a kitchen container
- Handwriting exemplars from John and Patsy Ramsey
- Duct tape and bindings from the victim
- A blanket used on victim and nightgown
- The wooden stick used on the garrote, broken off Patsy's paintbrush set in the basement, near the wine cellar
- JonBenét's clothing, including the shirt she'd worn to bed, found in her bathroom, and the shirt she'd worn that evening put back on her
- The broken basement window
- A scuff mark on the basement wall below the broken window
- The suitcase placed beneath the broken window
- An open cabinet near the victim's room with a package of diapers pulled out
- The location of the body
- The autopsy results

- Foreign DNA under the victim's fingernails and in her underwear
- Boot print in wine cellar
- A golf club found in the yard, with a blond hair on it.

Items specific to behavioral analysis include:

- Location of the body
- Night-time incident
- The victim covered with a blanket
- The victim was sexually violated
- The victim was both strangled and bludgeoned
- Unused nightgown near the victim's body
- The victim was last seen in her second-floor bedroom in a large, four-story house
- The other three members of the family had reported hearing nothing
- The stick used for the garrote was grabbed from a nearby box, not brought to the scene
- Knowledge that the window was broken because it was covered by a grate
- No sign of forced entry, no footprints in melting snow outside
- Pattern injuries on the body resembled those from a stun gun
- The wine cellar is a difficult room to find—so, familiarity with house layout
- Seemingly disguised printing for the ransom note
- Practice note, and possibly the start of a second practice note
- Language of the ransom note
- Practicing and writing the note inside the home, with materials found there

- Leaving a note although victim is dead and left inside home to be found
- Statements given by the parents/the 911 call
- Behavior of the parents during investigation— immediate representation by attorneys, the decision to first search the basement, the father's ability to see a child's body in the dark when another searcher had not, the removal of a number of items from JonBenét's room and clothing from the home

The ransom note proved to have been written on a tablet in the Ramsey home, with a pen from inside the home that was replaced back in its container, with evidence of making a few false starts.

 JonBenét had traveled widely, spending summers in Michigan where she participated in a variety of sports. Her mother had dyed her hair platinum for her participation in beauty pageants. She started these when she was four.

Patsy Ramsey, 39, had long kept a bedroom next to JonBenét's, as she suffered through chemotherapy for ovarian cancer, but by the time of the incident had returned to the master bedroom upstairs. She was the second wife for John Ramsey, 53, and they'd been married 16 years.

John Ramsey was a successful and wealthy CEO at a computer distribution company. A pilot and former military man, he was controlled and stoic throughout the investigation. He'd already experienced the loss of a 22-year-old daughter in an auto accident in 1992, and was the father of two other adult children, who'd been away from the house at the time.

The neighborhood and town where the Ramseys lived was an affluent, low-crime area, populated by luxury homes and estates.

During Christmas day, before the murder occurred, the family spent the morning opening gifts. They went to a friend's house for dinner, leaving there around 8:30 in the evening. They made two stops along the way home to drop off gifts at other friends' homes, arriving in their own home around 9:00. JonBenét had been carried to bed.

In terms of victimology, JonBenét was a 6-year-old female at home with her parents and older brother, Burke, in an affluent neighborhood. This environment put her at a very low risk for encountering a violence-prone stranger. The variable that increased her potential risk for encountering a stranger was her participation in beauty pageants, which increased her visibility and brought her into contact with many strangers. She stood out as she won awards and charmed audiences. It's possible that these public exposures may have drawn the unwanted attention of a child molester attending the pageants.

However, most child molesters are known to their victims and, instead of resorting to violence, they prefer using attention, affection and gifts to "seduce" a child over time. They typically snatch quickly and then transport the child to an area that they perceive to be safe for them to molest and/or murder the child. Any stranger entering the Ramsey home with the intent of doing harm would be at an elevated risk for detection, and the longer one spent inside the home, the greater the risk.

The offender wrote a 3-page ransom note, which was unusual not only for its length, but for a number of other issues. It was written inside the Ramsey home using a pad of paper and a pen from the home. The offender also had apparently started writing a "practice" ransom note on that same pad with that same pen. Most demand notes are written in advance in an area controlled by the offender. Many aspects of the phrasing used in the note made it less likely to have been written by a stranger.

Once finished concocting the demand note, the offender allegedly placed it on the back spiral staircase of the Ramsey home. Assuming the offender's goal was to have the note discovered so that the Ramseys could meet his financial demand, placing it on the back spiral staircase seems illogical unless one knew that the Ramseys routinely used that back staircase.

Ransom Note

The most incongruous decision that the offender made was to leave both the note and JonBenét's body inside the Ramseys' house. Any chance for obtaining the ransom money hinged on the offender being able to credibly guarantee JonBenét's safety. Once her body was found, no ransom would be paid and the note would be nothing other than potential physical evidence linking the author to the murder, as well as a behavioral clue that suggested an attempt to stage JonBenét's murder as a kidnapping.

It is important to note not only *where* the offender left the body but also *how* he left it. The offender wrapped JonBenét's body in a white blanket "papoose style" or, as John Ramsey stated, "...as if somebody were tucking her in..." and her favorite pink nightgown was laid next to the body. It is difficult to imagine that a stranger would know which nightgown was JonBenét's favorite and then spend time rummaging through the house in the dead of night looking for it. The careful wrapping of the body also suggests caring and concern for the victim. Collectively, these behaviors exhibited by the offender suggest a pre-existing relationship with the victim. Of interest is that JonBenét was still dressed in the clothing she had worn the day before, as was Patsy.

The autopsy further revealed no sexual assault, yet there was minor vaginal trauma. This would suggest a sexual motive for the crime, just as the demand note suggested a financial motive. Sexual assault seemed an unlikely motive as she was not sexually assaulted, and strangers who do so typically abduct the child to a place where it is safe for the offender to assault the child. It is so uncommon to attempt to sexually assault a child in her residence, with her parents and brother nearby, as to be improbable. In conclusion, the totality of the evidence is more consistent with an offender known to JonBenét—one who was comfortable in and familiar with the layout of the house—than it is with a stranger. The case remains unsolved today.

Apparently, some paranormal investigators believe that the place is haunted, probably due to this murder being unsolved. After all the publicity, it's easy to enter a house like this and "feel" sadness, or to use a ghost communication to get book sales, since there's small danger of being undermined by evidence. Everything needed for a story is out there in news items and books. A medium has only to be a good researcher to describe what a ghost might be saying. Nothing reported on "Haunting Evidence" provided a new lead or proof of anything. In fact, those who describe the ghost sightings seem unaware of most of the significant evidence, especially behavioral evidence. They probably don't expect their readers and viewers to know much more then superficial media accounts.

Florida

Some places seem to hold a lot of pent-up energy, especially where there are many victims and/or a great deal of suffering. The state-run segregated reform school, the Dozier School for Boys, closed its doors in Marianna in 2011 after over a century of existence. In retrospect, perhaps those doors should never have opened. Hundreds of orphans, homeless, aimless and criminal juveniles sent there, some as young as 5, have revealed stories of terrible abuse. They were chained up and tortured in a variety of ways. The "white house" was a small concrete building on the grounds where brutal beatings occurred. Boys would be tied to a bed before being repeatedly flogged with leather straps, often until they passed out. The records indicate at least 81 deaths, but the location of the graves of many of these unfortunates remains a mystery.

Florida's former Gov. Charlie Crist ordered a state investigation, but apparently investigators with the Florida Department of Law Enforcement were unable to find enough evidence to bring charges against anyone. They didn't take the word of residents who claimed to have seen boys literally die from the beatings or from being stuffed into large dryers, but they did find records of 81 deaths. By some reports, five died in a fire.

Dozier School for Boys. Florida State Archives.

A team of archaeologists and anthropologists from the University of South Florida undertook the task of searching for the missing. There's a small cemetery, but at least 50 of the decedents from the list are not buried there. The team used ground-penetrating radar over areas on the property that could hide unmarked graves and identified 49 gravesites. In September 2013, the state legislature approved the exhumation of 34 bodies from the cemetery. If enough of the skeletal remains are available for DNA analysis, the researchers can work up a biological profile to try to identify the boys. Several families who've lost a son, brother, uncle, or cousin are awaiting the results. Eventually, more exhumations may ensue.

It's not hard to see why ghost stories have surfaced, given the number of souls tormented over the years and the fact that many of the dead remain unidentified. To the school personnel, they were nobodies, apparently, but as human beings, they endured harsh conditions, neglect, loss, and torture before they expired.

Michigan

Evil Secrets

A bizarre secret is at the heart of this ghost story in the small community of Dixboro, not far from Ann Arbor. It dates back to 1835 when Martha Crawford, a widow, brought her young son from Canada to visit her sister Ann. Martha was smitten with Ann's brother-in-law, John Mulholland, and things soon progressed between them toward a possible wedding. But then Ann told Martha a secret about John that made her call everything off. Ann's husband, James, stepped in and told Ann that Martha must marry John. If she refused, she would die before she reached Canada.

The wedding took place, although the bride was terrified rather than ecstatic. Shortly thereafter, Ann died. Then John died. A feud ensued between Martha and James over John's house and property. The third death was Martha, but not before she had entrusted her physician, Dr. Sam Denton, with the secret. She made him promise that after she told him, he would bleed her until she died. He tricked her instead, but it wasn't long before she did meet her demise. Her 15-year-old son Joseph continued to live in the house.

In 1845, Joseph rented the house to Isaac van Woert and his family. They thought they were getting a nice house for raising their children, but Isaac soon learned otherwise.

One evening when he was in the yard, he looked through the window and saw a woman (not his wife) in a white nightdress, holding a candle. She moved slowly, as if in pain, and went into an upstairs bedroom. Isaac went inside. He thought he heard a bureau drawer open and shut in the room into which this woman had disappeared, but when he entered to find out who she was, everything was dark. No one was in the room.

Frightened, Isaac asked around and learned that Martha Mulholland had died in the house. There'd been talk of murder. It wasn't long before Isaac saw her again. He was in a bedroom and when he opened the door, he saw a light. It was 1:00 AM, so he was curious. He nearly ran right into the woman. Despite the light, he saw no candle. She seemed to be its source. She told him not to touch her.

Isaac stepped back, trembling. "What do you want?" he asked.

"He has got it," she said. "He robbed me little by little, until they kilt me. Now he has got it all!" She named her tormenter, James, and said that she wished her son would "come away." Apparently, she was afraid for his life. Then she disappeared.

This ghost's third appearance was in Isaac's bedroom. He woke up to find the room bathed in light. Again, the woman seemed to want her son to leave.

No one else in the family reported seeing this woman, but Isaac saw her again one evening after his wife and kids were in bed. She seemed to be reenacting her death. This time a man was with her whom Isaac knew, but the records of this visit fail to offer a name.

The ghost appeared to Isaac several more times. During one visit, she acted as if she'd been poisoned, possibly by the doctor. She seemed to implicate two men in her murder but never offered details. She referred to the "secret" and said that her husband, John, was a bad man. She also mentioned a well on the property but didn't reveal its significance.

Finally, Isaac moved his family out, but he went before a court to give his statement about what he'd seen. This inspired residents of Dixboro to exhume Martha's body. At the coroner's inquest in 1846, the cause of death was found to be poisoning. The doctor was suspected as an accomplice with James Mulholland, who quickly left the area, abandoning everything. His property was sold at a sheriff's auction. Joseph remained in Dixboro. Some time between 1860 and 1870, the haunted house burned to the ground.

The terrible secret was never discovered. However, it was known that before Martha and Joseph arrived, a traveling tin peddler had disappeared while staying at an inn that stood on Mulholland property. Because Martha had kept referring to the well, townspeople wondered if John or James, or both, had murdered the man and dumped him down the well. No body or other suspicions items were found in the well, but ghost legends arose that on a cold, still night, one can hear the faint chimes of a peddler's bell.

Since the ghost in this haunting seemed to be (at least in the past) very willing to appear and speak to the living *without* the aid of modern ghost hunting devices or techniques, this would be a classic case to re-open paranormally. As well, there seems to be a dreadful secret, first passed to Martha by Ann, then from Martha to her physician.

A visit to Dixboro and the site of the house would be helpful. Since the names of the participants are known, attempts at gathering EVP may yield the secret. In addition, dowsing rods and pendulum work could also gather information. The fact that the ghost (presumably Martha) apparently did not reveal the secret to Isaac doesn't mean that she didn't try. Isaac may have misunderstood what she was saying or doing because he was expecting something else indicating possible confirmation bias.

Dowsing rods could be used to find the old well or burials on the site. EVP techniques could be utilized to record the sound of the peddler's bell, just as it has successfully recorded bits of Civil War Era music in Gettysburg.

The Long Reunion

Jackson, Michigan, is in the central part of the Lower Peninsula. It has a famous cemetery where people sometimes still go during the night of November 21 to see a strange ghostly reunion between a murdered man and his daughter. Perhaps that's because the murders remain unsolved.

Jackson was a much smaller town in 1883 than it is today, and this assault was extreme. On the night of November 21, there was a violent thunderstorm. Its noise buffered the sound of bullets that killed four people in their sleep in the Jacob Crouch house. Jacob, 74, was one of the victims, along with his eight-months-pregnant daughter, Eunice White, her husband, and a visitor from Pennsylvania named Moses Polley.

As horrendous as this massacre was, it was apparently just the start. Two months later, Jacob's other daughter, Susan Holcomb, appeared to have been poisoned in her home. Then Crouch's former hired hand, James Fay, died shortly after. Despite the evidence of murder, his death was declared a suicide. With six people dead (seven, if the unborn child was included), the local residents were pretty rattled.

George Bolles, a 16-year-old black farmhand, had discovered the bodies. He'd seen a man outside during the storm holding a lantern and thought he'd heard a scream that had sent him into hiding. The next day when he saw what had happened in the house, he went for help. Jacob had been shot in the head, as was Polley, while Eunice had taken four bullets and her husband two. The Jackson County asked a photographer to get a likeness of Eunice White's eyes to see if the image of her killer was still reflected in them (a common notion in those days). Apparently, it wasn't.

MRS. EUNICE WHITE.   HENRY WHITE.

JACOB CROUCH.   MOSES POLLEY.

One theory held that Jacob, a wealthy wheat farmer who owned 1,000 acres, had planned to leave his fortune to Eunice's unborn child and cut his grown children out of his will. Besides Susan, he had two sons, Judd and Byron. Rumors arose that Byron had hired a band of Texas cowboys to kill his father and the others. Yet even with the Pinkerton Detective agency on the case, nothing of merit turned up.

By March, Judd Crouch and Daniel Holcomb, Susan's husband, were charged with the murders. Daniel's trial started November 8, 1884. Prosecutor Frank Hewlett, who was in poor health, died during the trial. (During the trial, a witness was also killed by her ax-wielding husband.) All evidence offered was circumstantial. There were no witnesses to the shooting, so the jury returned a verdict of not guilty. Judd Crouch was never brought to trial. In 1886, three bloody shirts were found buried inside the stump of a tree on the Holcomb property, but to whom they belonged remained a mystery.

Now for the ghost story: The victims had been buried in different cemeteries. Jacob ended up where his wife had been buried years before on the corner of Horton and Reynolds Road, a mile from his home. Eunice and her husband were buried in St. John's Cemetery five miles away. A legend developed that on the anniversary of the slaughter each year, Eunice wanted to be near her father, so her spirit would be seen moving along the five-mile route to join him. Some reports said their ghostly forms embraced.

Obviously, such stories draw ghost hunters, and several groups claim to have caught images of an ectoplasmic substance floating toward Jacob's grave on the night in question. (However, late November in Michigan is generally quite cold, and breath caught on film sometimes resembles ectoplasm.) It's easy enough to go set up near this small cemetery on the specific night, should anyone wish to test the tales.

New Jersey

Cold Companion

On the Douglass campus at Rutgers University, a case of entity possession during the 1960s got some attention. A student living in Woodbury Hall suddenly began to have nightmares of a ghost wrapped in a shroud that seemed to be wrapped around her. She believed it was trying to steal her soul. She lost sleep and attempted to escape by going home, but the specter seemed to follow her, as if it was attached to her.

The ghost apparently revealed her identity one day: she was the spirit of Mary Lacey from Andover, Massachusetts. Although condemned during the Salem witch trials to hang, she had won release by betraying others. After she'd died, she'd been tormented by the lies she'd told that had led to innocent people dying.

The student kept assuring her that she'd been forgiven and eventually, this entity faded away.

North Carolina

Which Victim is the Ghost?

There are many tales about the infamous pirate, Blackbeard, who had several places in North Carolina. One was on Ocracoke Island, but another is in Beaufort. He had a large white house on Taylor Creek, with an inlet to the Atlantic Ocean. Today this house, the oldest in Beaufort, is called the Hammock House.

Blackbeard took residence here for a while with a woman he called his wife. She was just 18 and appeared to be his captive. The stories say that one day he grew angry with her and hanged her from an oak tree in the backyard. Supposedly, her ghost lingers, screaming at times in agony.

Other tales are told of violent deaths in the home, along with the story of men who were preparing for construction in 1915 finding the remains of three missing Yankee soldiers buried near the back porch. Apparently when they stayed here, they were murdered.

Paranormal Forces and Aggressive Spirits

Entities

About a week before serial killer Ted Bundy abducted and murdered two girls on the same day in Washington State, he'd seemed odd to his girlfriend. Later she would say that he'd pushed her out of a raft into icy water and made no move to help her. "His face had gone blank," she stated, "as though he was not there at all. I had a sense that he wasn't seeing me."

Others had seen something similar, and Bundy seemed to think it was a force that sometimes took him over. To several interviewers after Bundy's arrest, he described an "entity" that emerged from him whenever he was tense or drunk. Defense investigator Joe Aloi got a clear view. As they talked, he noticed an odor suddenly emanate from Bundy. Then Bundy's face and body contorted.

"I felt that negative electricity," Aloi said, "and along with that came that smell." Aloi thought Bundy might try to kill him. (Other interrogators say this is adrenaline-generated sweat, so perhaps it wasn't so unique.)

Bundy said that during his encounters with victims, "the entity" took over, looking for satisfaction. It was not an alter-personality, he insisted, but more like a disordered part of him. A psychiatrist disagreed, diagnosing him as bipolar and a possible multiple personality (but she was the only mental health expert who did so).

In third-person, Bundy described his experience: "What began to happen was that ... important matters were not being rearranged or [were] otherwise interfered with by this voyeuristic behavior, but with increasing regularity, things were postponed or otherwise rescheduled, to, uh, work around, uh, hours and hours spent on the street, at night and during the early morning hours...

"And as the condition develops and its purposes or its characteristics become more well defined, it begins to demand more time of the individual ... There's a certain amount of tension, uh, struggle, between the normal personality and this, this, uh, psychopathological, uh, entity ... The tension between normal individual, uh, normal consciousness of this individual and those demands being submitted to him via this competing ... this condition inside him seems to be competing for more attention..."

It was an independent thing, he insisted, because the entity and his own personality were active at the same time. He'd notice tension building and the entity would break through. It would demand to act out violently, and then Bundy would drink and lose his inhibitions. At this point, he lost all control. The entity took over. Bundy said that it only happened when he was considerably intoxicated.

One evening, when he was drunk, he saw a woman leave a bar alone. He followed her until she turned into a dark street. This was easy pickings.

"The urge to do something to that person seized him—in a way he'd never been affected before ... and it seized him strongly. And to the point where, uh, without giving a great deal of thought, he searched around for some instrumentality to uh, uh, attack this woman with."

Often, Bundy would prepare for a victim. For example, he removed the passenger side seat in order to shove a body into that space after he'd clunked a woman with a tire iron. Thus, it wasn't that he was totally helpless to this entity. He knew its hunger and he knew that drinking a lot would encourage him to seek another victim. He had control over these things and he made antisocial choices. He grew addicted to the excitement of sexual assault and murder, but he admitted that he always had to be pretty wasted.

*   *   *

H. H. Holmes was arrested for a murder he committed as part of an insurance scam in Philadelphia. Investigators soon realized that this con man had murdered quite a number of people over the years, including several children. Herman Webster Mudgett, a.k.a., H. H. Holmes, had built a hotel—his "castle"—in Chicago during the development of the 1893 World's Fair. He'd rent rooms to young ladies, lock them in and gas them to death. He'd slide the bodies down specially built chutes to the cellar where he'd installed a massive furnace. He'd either burn them to ash, dissolve them in a vat of acid, or strip the flesh from their bones to sell their skeletons to medical schools.

In prison, facing execution, Holmes aimed to beef up his reputation as the most notorious killer in the world. In an illustrated confession that took up four full newsprint pages, he claimed to have killed more than 100 people. Apparently having second thoughts, he reduced this number to 27.

Holmes insisted that he could not help what he'd done. He was born to be vile. "I was born with the Evil One as my sponsor beside the bed where I was ushered into the world," he lamented. "It now seems a fitting time, if ever, to make known the details of the twenty-seven murders, of which it would be useless to longer say I am not guilty."

As he admitted to the murders, he said he was "thus branding myself as the most detestable criminal of modern times." He thought his countenance was changing as he sat in prison, and that he looked more satanic. "I have become afflicted with that dread disease, rare but terrible...a malformation.... My head and face are gradually assuming an elongated shape. I believe fully that I am growing to resemble the devil—that the similitude is almost completed."

By the time Holmes went to trial, he'd become considerably less melodramatic. He'd even recanted his confessions. But there was plenty of evidence for the fraud-murder in Philadelphia and Holmes was convicted and executed by hanging. How many people he ultimately murdered remains a matter of conjecture.

*   *   *

"Gainesville Ripper" Danny Rolling said he'd been under the influence of a demon called "Gemini" when he committed five murders in Florida during the summer of 1990. The first crime scene involved two freshmen at the University of Florida who'd been repeatedly stabbed, mutilated and posed for shocking effect. Investigators soon found the nude, mutilated body of an 18-year-old in her bedroom: her head was propped on a bookshelf. Two students, one male and one female, were found dead in their apartment two days later,

Arrested, Rolling resorted to the "Gemini" excuse. Investigators learned that he was referring to a fictional creature from a 1990 film, Exorcist III. Based on the original film, The Exorcist, the plot features a demon seeking possession of a human that had migrated into a wandering lunatic, who was locked up. Fifteen years later, Gemini emerges again to force the body he "owns" to start killing. His favorite method is to paralyze his victims with the drug succinlycholine, which leaves them alert and aware of their torture.

Rolling's diminished capacity ploy failed to work. He was convicted.

*   *   *

Then there was "BTK," Dennis Rader, who murdered ten people in Kansas between 1974 and 1991. At one point during the investigation, in an effort to get attention, Rader had anonymously called a reporter at the Wichita Eagle and instructed him to go to the public library. There, he should look inside *Applied Engineering Mechanics*. There would be a letter detailing his slaughter of a family of four (the Oteros in 1974, his first murders). Also in this disjointed note, the offender said he'd studied the habits of other sexual criminals and had a "monster" in his brain that compelled him to kill: "The pressure is great and some-times he run the game to his liking." BTK indicated that this monster had "already chosen his next victim."

Even today in his solitary prison cell, Rader muses over whether he was possessed by a demon. The pastor of his church was certain of it and probably influenced Rader to consider this possibility.

*   *   *

Sean Richard Sellers, just 16, brought vials of blood to school and drank them in front of other students. He also quoted from the Satanic Bible. He'd spent hours performing rituals in his bedroom, using his own blood to write notes to Satan. Eventually he decided to prove he could exercise the ultimate power over someone: with murder.

On September 8, 1985, Sellers entered a convenience store and fatally shot the clerk. That was just for practice. Not long afterward, Sellers waited until his parents were asleep. Then he dressed in a ritualistic manner in black underwear before walking into their bedroom to shoot them both.

After he was charged with the murders, he said that dreams about blood had influenced him. "Demons were the beings that would do things I wanted done," he wrote in his confession. "They were the keys to the power Satanism promised." Sellers said that when his courage nearly failed him, he reverted to a "cold, determined, heartless and evil" personality. "When I was that person, that murderer, I felt superior."

*   *   *

Gary Gilmore's mother, Bessie, claimed to have seen an entity that she believed influenced Gary to become a killer. Bessie had a deep-rooted superstition that went back to her own childhood. She believed that as a girl playing with a Ouija board, she had conjured up a demon that had attached itself to her family. When one of her sisters was killed and another paralyzed in an accident, she felt certain it was the demon's work.

After she married, she learned that her mother-in-law, Fay, was a medium who reportedly could persuade spirits to materialize. One night when Bessie and her sons were staying with Fay, she conducted a séance to contact the spirit of a suspected murderer. Later that night, Bessie woke up to the feeling of being touched, and when she turned over, she claimed she was looking into the face of a leering inhuman creature. She jumped out of bed and saw Fay, an invalid, on her feet and staggering toward her, insisting that she get out *now*.

Bessie ran to Gary's room and saw the demon leaning over her son, staring into his eyes. She grabbed the kids and ran.

Back at home Gary began to have terrible, shuddering nightmares that he was being beheaded. He was often certain something was in the room with him, trying to get him. Headaches plagued him for the rest of his life. Although Gary never blamed a demon for his murder spree, his mother believed to her dying day that the thing had taken over her son's soul and turned him into a killer.

Mental State

The legal system is based in the idea that people are rational agents who freely choose their actions and are therefore both responsible and punishable. However, mental health professionals are just as sure that a significant part of human behavior is conditioned by factors beyond one's control or awareness. Although a person may have the *actus reus* (ability to commit the act) he or she might not possess the *mens rea* (ability to intend the act, appreciate its wrongfulness, and/or to foresee the act's consequences). Both conditions are required to find a person criminally responsible.

Demonologists and paranormalists also believe that forces might be involved in an offender's violence, which would diminish his or her *mens rea.*

However, how can we tell whether it's spiritual or psychological? Extreme mental illness involves bizarre and disturbed emotions, behaviors, thoughts, and beliefs that may interfere with a person's ability to function in work and relationships; it often isolates the person. In severe forms, it can make people dangerous to others and/or themselves. The most prevalent of the psychotic disorders, schizophrenia, is marked by a confusion of thinking and speech that is at times chronic. It occurs equally in men and women, and generally appears between the ages of fifteen and thirty-five. There appears to be a significant genetic component, in that a person may inherit a tendency toward it that can be triggered by an outside stressor. It also responds to medication. This would support a biological basis for the behavior.

Another mental disorder that can produce psychotic episodes is bipolar affective disorder, formerly manic-depressive disorder. It is a cyclical disturbance characterized by dramatic mood swings between mania and depression. People suffering from it might experience intense periods of high energy in which they feel superhuman. They go without rest for long periods of time, have grandiose ideas, and accomplish an astonishing amount of work. However, they might then swing into serious depression, sometimes accompanied by delusions and thoughts of suicide. They might hear voices during either phase, but between phases, they would generally feel normal. This condition, too, responds to medication.

Finally, we have dissociative identity disorder (DID), formally known as multiple personality disorder. It's commonly been confused with schizophrenia as a split personality. The idea of DID is that a person has fractured into several alter personalities and that two or more sub-personalities share a single body, each with its own identity and each taking turns controlling the personality and behavior. They're believed to emerge as a result of trauma (even this is disputed), such as sexual abuse and they usually emerge before the age of five. To some extent, as some experts have written, the "alters" arise to protect the "core personality" from overwhelming memories. Some alters appear to form from forbidden impulses as well.

Experts indicate that a traumatic memory that is not recalled might still have the energy to emerge in symptoms like depression, numbness, hypersensitivity, and reactions to certain environmental triggers that can touch on that memory. There may also be vague flashbacks. These people might "trance out," feel out of touch with reality, ignore genuine pain, and experience sudden panic attacks. They might also develop eating disorders and other addictions, and abuse others or themselves. Generally, they have trouble with intimacy and can experience any number of sexual dysfunctions and sleep disturbances.

Then, there's the other side. Some people believe that serial killers are demon-possessed. Especially those who claim to have the experience of alter personalities. Katherine described Bundy's experience to Rosemary Ellen Guiley, one of the leading experts on the paranormal today. Rosemary has published over 50 books on a wide range of paranormal, spiritual, and mystical topics. She's been working pretty much full-time in the paranormal realm since 1983, as a researcher and investigator. You can ask her about any paranormal topic from angels to demons. Since she had researched the Djinn, a species of entity like what some of these killers have described, we asked her to tell us about it.

"In early Arabian lore," Rosemary said, "the Djinn originated out of the winds. The Qur'an says Allah created them out of smokeless fire, and the angels out of a pure spiritual light. We perceive angels, Djinn, fairies, demons, ETs and even Bigfoot as having human-like hierarchies and social structures, but whether they really do or this is a human projection is not certain.

"Supposedly there are give-away signs. In old Djinn lore, they could not duplicate 100 percent of a human body, and usually their animal-like, hairy legs and feet gave them away. I have speculated that Shadow People wear hats and cowls to cover up imperfect heads. Some experiencers say the eyes of the human-shaped Djinn will shift to odd colors or a reptilian appearance. I believe the Djinn and other shape-shifters are among us every day, and we never know unless we have certain experiences with them.

"According to lore, the Djinn were here first and were pushed out by or for us, and some of them are still angry about it and want the place back. Their motives include curiosity, infatuation, obsession, playfulness, trickiness, hostility, and malevolence. Some people feel Djinn are benevolent and helpful, but if they are, it is always for a price. People have a tendency to think that other entities are like cutout cookies, all the same. The Djinn (as well as other beings) are varied, like humans, neither all good nor all bad, and with unique personalities.

"The entity that Ted Bundy described as having an influence on his murderous behavior could very well have been a Djinn. In Djinn lore, every person is born with a Djinn that stays with the person for their entire life. Like the

Greek daimon, the Djinn can be either good or bad, and it will influence a person accordingly.

"A bad or evil Djinn understands the person's weaknesses and takes advantage of them in a type of possession. Its means of influence can include a voice in the head, dreams, and thoughts and urges that arise. It would be capable of creating a physical tension or pressure that would build until released by action – in Bundy's case, killing. And, it would be relentless, pushing and pushing until the person went over the edge. Defense investigator Joe Aloi noticed dramatic changes in Bundy: contortions of the face and body, an unpleasant odor, and 'negative electricity.' All of these would be consistent with Djinn possession.

"When the Djinn gains the upper hand, it distorts the person's body, especially the face. Foul odors are common. The description of negative electricity is especially interesting, for the Djinn are said to be made of 'smokeless fire,' perhaps a type of plasma, and they often give off an electrical presence when they manifest."

Still, we've come across an intriguing alternate explanation.

In 2006, an article was published in the prestigious journal *Nature* about how Swiss neuroscientists had stimulated an area of a patient's brain, inducing some of the same effects people claim to feel in haunted spaces. The subject was 22 and had no history of psychiatric disorders or delusions. During their examination of her prior to surgery for epilepsy, they stimulated the left junction of her temporo-parietal lobe. She said she had an impression of a solid figure standing behind her, but no one was there. She described him as young, silent, and posing as if to mirror her position. It felt disturbing.

The doctors urged the patient to sit up and they stimulated her brain once again. This time, she said, the figure had wrapped his arms around her, just like the way she had her arms around her knees. Taken together, these experiences suggested that her brain was using her body to create a phantom presence.

In another test, she held a card in her right hand, and after stimulation in the same area, she again reported the shadow person, but this time she had a stronger impression of a personality. She knew what he wanted. "He wants to take the card," she said. "He doesn't want me to read." The doctors weren't sure what to make of this.

It seems possible that when some of these offenders who aren't just malingering are in a highly aroused state, some wiring in their brain gives them a similar experience of a shadow person or entity close at hand. This wouldn't explain what Bessie Gilmore supposedly witnessed, but it could be implicated in BTK's "monster," Bundy's entity, and other "dark passenger" descriptions.

Another Possibility

Besides demon and Djinn possession, there is another possibility for criminal activity that comes from the spirit world: a walk-in.

A walk-in is the spiritual take-over of an individual's body by the spirit of another deceased individual. Some sources indicate that it is a consensual take-over of the body where the two souls mutually decide to exchange places. The incoming spirit moves into the body while the outgoing spirit moves on to fulfill its destiny. The outgoing spirit usually must give permission for the walk-in to occur. It has also been called soul transference.

A walk-in often occurs after a traumatic experience to the body—an accident, illness, surgery or other physical assault on the body. Some sources say that a walk-in occurs when the original body/spirit is vulnerable—during alcoholism, mental illness, drug addiction or emotional distress. This leads to the theory that a walk-in isn't necessarily a welcome thing.

A complete, if only subtle, change in the person experiencing the walk-in is observed. They are interested or obsessed with things that never interested them before. They gather new friends and ignore old ones. They take up new hobbies and relinquish old habits. They feel like a different person, sometimes not recognizing old acquaintances or perhaps remembering former habitats.

It is also theorized that if the entity walking in is evil, the person experiencing the walk-in is changed for the worse and may begin aberrant behaviors.

Haunted Crime Scene Investigations

The Mysterious Ink Blot

In *Blood & Ghosts*, we included a story told to Katherine by a forensic chemist about a mysterious splotch of ink that he'd analyzed. Then we saw the rest of the story in a documentary that Paul Davids made, so we're redelivering this tale to readers as Paul Davids told it. It wasn't quite like Katherine had heard from the chemist (who also appears in the documentary), so this narrative rectifies some errors. It also raises some key ideas about careful procedures and about powers from the Other Side.

Forrest I. Ackerman

In *The Life After Death Project*, Paul Davids talks about being a close associate of Forrest J. Ackerman, who founded the magazine, *Famous Monsters of Filmland*. "Forry's" home had been a veritable museum of horror films, figurines, and books. Davids had won a contest that Ackerman had offered in the magazine and over the years, they'd become good friends. When Forrest died, Davids spoke at his memorial tribute in March 2009. Then something odd happened on March 18 at 8:30 in the evening.

Davids was at his home in Santa Fe, New Mexico, and had started printing documents that he needed for taxes. He left the printer running while he left the room. When he returned, he glanced at the documents. They looked fine, so he tossed them on the bed.

A little later he retrieved them. He noticed something odd on one page that he hadn't seen before: an ink-like substance, still wet, had obliterated one line that contained four words. It was as if someone had drawn a brush over those words. He could see through the ink to read "Spoke to," but the following two words—seemingly a name—were under ink that was more opaque.

Davids looked around to try to discover the source of the liquid. It wasn't from the printer, because he'd looked at the document before placing it on the bed and it had been clear. There were no leaks from the ceiling and he hadn't taken the documents into the bathroom or brought anything that leaked or dripped into the bedroom. Davids was home alone, so no one had come in to disturb anything during the time that he was out of the room. There were no pets.

He looked at the original file and realized that the obliterated name was Joe Amodei, which meant nothing to him. He talked to his acquaintances and learned that other odd things had occurred around the time of Ackerman's death, most of which had captured Forry's unique sense of humor. A team of filmmakers from Canada had visited Ackerman's vault at, of all places, *Forest* Lawn cemetery. They'd knocked on it and "talked" to him. When they returned to their rooms, they'd experienced several issues with their computers. For example, they were going onto a Facebook site for Ackerman. To get to it they had to type letters and numbers into a box intended to filter out SPAM. Oddly enough, the code that allowed them entry was Ackerman000, which they were not able to replicate. Yet they knew that Ackerman did not believe in an afterlife.

Davids recalled that when he'd won the contest back when he was 14, Ackerman had sent him a letter with five stamps. One had featured Edgar Allan Poe and the other four showed the Palace of Governors on the central plaza in Santa Fe—the very town in which the words had been obliterated on his document. But who was this Amodei?

Davids knew that Ackerman loved wordplay, especially with names, so he called Ackerman's assistant, Joe Moe, and then realized that the obliterated name might point to Joe. "Amodei" contained "Moe" in it. Sort of. Davids then learned that, directly after Ackerman's death, Moe had dreamed of Ackerman coming to him and commenting positively on the tribute at which Davids had spoken.

Davids decided to ask a scientist about the ink on the document. He contacted Dr. Jay Siegel, chair of the chemistry department at Indiana University. Davids delivered the document in person. Siegel examined it and said that the obliteration was not the result of an accidental drip. What he'd first thought were paintbrush strokes turned out to be paper fibers, but he thought the obliteration had been targeted to those four words. He performed an analysis that dissolved the printer ink, but it failed to work on the obliterating ink. While they were working on it, a computer across the room turned on by itself, startling them.

Siegel decided to get a colleague involved, Professor John Allison, a forensic chemist in New Jersey. (This is the story we told in *Blood & Ghosts*.) Intrigued, Allison examined the paper. The obliteration was a bluish substance on top of black printer's ink. He tried a number of tests on the paper, but he could not recreate the obliteration. He did find foreign elements, such as silver and something he could not identify, so he applied laser desorption mass spectrometry. However, no source in Davids' home matched the foreign elements.

During the time in which the document was undergoing this examination, several odd things occurred. One involved an unwound clock suddenly chiming at the moment Allison was discussing the document with someone. Allison also said that he'd once placed the document under his briefcase on a chair. When he came back, the papers were on the floor, spread out. There was no fan in the room and no source to account for how the document had come loose. Allison could not replicate the position of the pages when he tried to knock them off the chair. It was as if someone had deliberately spread them out on the floor.

However, despite the application of sophisticated tests, the mystery remained unsolved. If Ackerman *was* around, he apparently could not make his presence more clearly known. Even so, this is a case of paranormal forensics: an odd incident to which some of the best tests in forensic chemistry were diligently applied, with controls. Both scientists admitted on camera to being mystified. However, the attempt to make "Amodei" into something more meaningful in the context of Ackerman is the sort of thing that undermines credibility for paranormalists. It's among Holmes's errors of thinking. It's as if they must find a way to make an unusual event into a supernatural one, so they twist things until it sounds good. That's a mix of cherry picking, wishful thinking, and confirmation bias.

The Black Dahlia

The famous dismemberment murder of Elizabeth Short remains unsolved and has been revisited by true crime and paranormalists alike. About twelve years ago, Katherine researched the case for former FBI profiler John Douglas (*The Cases that Haunt Us*), and later for a profile done by former FBI profiler Gregg McCrary for The Crime Library, which gave her first-hand knowledge of a professional behavioral assessment.

Below is the basic story, McCrary's interpretation, a ghost hunting group's analysis, and our summary, with a suggestion for how we would use all sources of information before drawing our own conclusions.

On 39th and Norton in the Leimert Park area of Los Angeles, Betty Bersinger noticed the dismembered nude body of a dark-haired young woman in a vacant weedy lot. It was around mid-morning on January 15, 1947.

The body had been drained of blood, so its skin was a stark white against the dark grass. It had been dumped after the dew had settled but before dawn, while the grass was still wet. By this time, murder victim Elizabeth Short, 22, had been dead approximately ten hours. Due to a lack of blood and other items, it was clear that she'd been killed and mutilated elsewhere. In fact, she'd been cut in half.

As police arrived and questioned witnesses, they learned about a black sedan, possibly a Ford, with mud spattered on a front fender, creeping along the driveway of the vacant lot around 6:00 A.M. No one could describe the driver.

Most significant for a behavioral analysis of the unknown offender were the condition and position of the body. Short was left sexually posed, on her back with her arms raised over her shoulders, her elbows bent, and her legs spread wide apart. She'd been sliced in half at the waist, and the two parts were carefully placed in a linear alignment, with a ten-inch gap. Her face and breasts had been badly slashed, and rope marks on her wrists, ankles, and neck indicated that, at some point, she'd been bound. A section of her left leg had been cut deeply through the muscles, and a large piece of muscle and skin was missing from that area. Pubic hairs appear to have been pulled or cut out, and there were deep slashes from her mouth running along both sides of her face. The lower torso was angled upward at the hips, leading the medical examiner to believe that this young woman had been in a semi-recumbent position at the time of death and the corpse had stiffened in this position.

From the damp hair and lack of blood, it appeared as though she'd been washed clean. Her fingerprint ridges appeared shrunken and the skin of the fingers had puckered into grooves, as if she'd been kept on ice. Quite simply, it was a bizarre case, and it would grow even stranger as the investigation unfolded.

The coroner found that the cause of death was from "hemorrhage and shock due to concussion of the brain and lacerations of the face." There were multiple lacerations to the mid-forehead, right forehead, and top of the head. There were also multiple crisscross lacerations in the pubic area, and stab wounds into the intestine and both kidneys. Short had not been pregnant, but within the vagina, which reportedly was not fully formed (this has been disputed in recent years), the pathologist found a piece of skin with subcutaneous tissue attached. On it was several crisscrossing lacerations.

It appeared that the victim had been anally penetrated after death as well, and inside the anal canal was a tuft of brown curly hair, which bore similarities to the victim's pubic hair. The stomach was filled with feces, but there was no sperm in any orifice.

What Gregg McCrary could tell about the offender was this: he or she (most likely he) murdered Short in a place that was under his control, where he was unconcerned about being interrupted. There, he'd spent considerable time torturing, assaulting, murdering and mutilating the victim. He had access to ice or an "ice box" in which he kept the body for a brief period. This was probably instrumental to something else, such as complicating time-of-death estimates, and not part of a ritual.

The rope marks are consistent with instrumental restraints. It was probably to keep her under control.

There are indications, McCrary added, that this offender was sexually sadistic. It's likely that the multiple tiny abrasions and lacerations were ante-mortem. If her pubic hair was pulled before death rather than cut afterward, this would be sadistic as well. Cutting it to stuff into a body cavity indicated a need to degrade and humiliate; feces in her stomach confirmed this possibility.

The lack of blood in the body suggests that Short was alive when this offender inflicted the multiple injuries. Assault on sexually significant areas is also consistent with a sexually sadistic offender.

The amount of time the offender spent with the victim, as evidenced by the ante-mortem and post-mortem assaults followed by the washing of the body, is consistent with an offender who not only lives alone, but is also comfortable around bodies and has probably murdered before. The manner in which the offender disposed of the body indicated that he wanted (or needed) not only to display the body publicly, but to do so in a manner that was degrading and contemptuous.

If he selected the specific dump area because on a map it resembled the female genital area (as some suggest), then he may have thought about such a crime before and considered what he would do with the body as part of his own private game.

The reports of a black sedan, crawling around the area may or may not be of significance. It could be a "red herring," so it's important to not let it sidetrack us.

To understand this crime, we need to know about the victim, especially if there is evidence that the offender knew her rather than randomly grabbing her off the street. The brutalization and post-mortem humiliation suggests that he probably did know her or was at least acquainted with her.

We cannot overestimate the importance of victimology, the comprehensive study of the victim(s). The goal is to accurately place the victim(s) along a risk continuum from low to moderate to high, and to calculate whom the victim(s) might have encountered. This analysis is accomplished by conducting an investigation of victim situational and lifestyle variables. We want to determine what might have elevated an individual's potential for being the victim of violence.

Known risk factors include involvement in criminal activity, severely strained personal relationships, financial problems, and drug use. Once risk factors are identified, they must be integrated with the analysis of all forensic and behavioral evidence in an effort to develop potential motives.

During victimology, homicides are worked from the inside (the victim) out in concentric spheres. The first sphere typically includes immediate family members, intimate partners, etc. The next sphere includes friends, associates, co-workers, former partners, neighbors, and distant relatives. The least likely scenario, on the outside circle, is a stranger-based homicide. While those clearly occur, investigators should not leap first to this hypothesis. Rather, they should work their way by painstakingly investigating and eliminating those closest to the victim first, especially anyone who might harbor a motive to harm.

So, on to the victim. Elizabeth Short was born in Hyde Park, Massachusetts, on July 29, 1924. She came to Hollywood to break into the movie business and worked to position herself in the "right" networks. She gained a reputation as a tease that would perform oral sex. Short liked to socialize and loved the Hollywood nightlife. One of her friends, a radio ad salesman named Hal McGuire told a story that was typical of the many impressions people had of her:

"Her manner was that she could be friends with you right from the start—guys as well as girls—only with the guys, I guess, they felt that right away there was interest on her part in them as boyfriends, but in fact, you quickly learned that wasn't what she had in mind. It was more like you'd been at a church social or a girl scout meeting—What you had was this beautiful girl that would light up so bright when she saw you, sort of caught you off guard, and had you thinking she'd taken a turn for you. When you saw that wasn't the case, it was pretty disappointing."

Her neediness and her availability made her a higher risk victim. She depended on others and seemed almost to be homeless. She tended to go with whoever was willing to give her a place to stay. In addition, she wanted to advance herself, so she apparently used people. It's likely that some people became angry with her, or that she met a psychopathic predator.

Not long after her death, the Los Angeles *Examiner* received a package with a note created from newspaper lettering that said, "Here is Dahlia's Belongings," and "Letter to Follow." Inside the package were Short's social security card, birth certificate, a telegram, photographs with various servicemen, business cards, a newspaper clipping of a man whom Short had passed off as her deceased husband, and claim checks for the suitcases she had left at the bus depot. Another item was an address book with around 75 names and addresses, but with several pages recently torn out—another indication that her killer had known her. That she was clearly a liar also raised her risk. In addition, it's likely she owed people money—perhaps a lot of money.

Handwriting Expert Henry Silver
LA Public Library/Herald-Examiner Collection

On January 26, a woman's purse and black suede shoes, identified as Short's, were located at a garbage dump on East 25th Street. This indicated that the killer was traveling north from the body dumpsite. It might show approximately where the murder occurred, since he could have been returning to clean it up.

On January 27, a dealer in second-hand clothing on Santa Monica Boulevard received a phone call from a man who had women's clothing to sell. He instructed the dealer to come to 1842 North Cherokee, apartment 501. The dealer declined and realized too late that this was one of Short's former addresses.

In brief, McCrary speculated, the person who killed Elizabeth Short had to have access to a place and have some criminal sophistication. He was probably older than her and would not have been panicked over killing her. He was angry, but it was a controlled rage. He was able to form a plan and carry it out. We can see that he's not just a random killer; to kill again, he'd need a similar context. He's not just striking out. There are certain criteria that his victims had to meet, and certain circumstances.

Short's Ghost?

Reportedly, the ghost of Elizabeth Short has been seen at the Biltmore Hotel in Los Angeles, where she was last seen alive after a man dropped her off. Police had learned of Robert "Red" Manley, 25, a hardware salesman that Short had met in San Diego. Manley had contemplated having an affair with her. He'd first met her on December 15th and had then returned to look for her. On January 8, he picked her up from where she was staying and paid for a room for her for that night. They went out together to different nightspots and returned to the motel. Manley slept on the bed, while Short, complaining of illness, slept in a chair.

She told Manley, he later told police that she was going back home to Boston but first she was going to meet her sister at the Biltmore Hotel. She checked her luggage at the Greyhound depot and they went to Los Angeles. Manley had to leave at 6:30 that evening, so he dropped her off at the hotel. That's the last he saw her.

Hotel staff saw her making phone calls. She waited a while, as if she expected someone to pick her up, and finally, near 10:00 P.M., she left. She was wearing a collarless black suit, a frilly white blouse, black suede shoes, white gloves, and a full-length beige coat. No one saw whoever might have picked her up.

But these are not the clothes she wears as a ghost. Always dressed in black, she lingers in the lobby, outside, or on the elevator, apparently going to the 6th floor.

The "Black Dahlia" case is among the most famous of Hollywood murders. It was featured on a paranormal TV series, *Haunted Encounters*, investigated by the "Paranormal Syndicate." This group had accepted as fact a theory from former LAPD homicide detective Steve Hodel.

In 2003, Hodel published a book claiming his father, who had died a decade earlier, had committed the Black Dahlia murder, along with a number of others. Hodel based this primarily on two pictures in his deceased father's photo album that Hodel believes resemble Short. He weaves an elaborate story around this evidence.

However, Short's family insists the photos are not of her. Other observers agree, and in fact, Hodel actually located and identified one of the photographic subjects as a former friend of his father's. A woman he believed was Short apparently was not.

In a report to the grand jury on February 20, 1951, Lt. Frank Jemison of the LA County DA's office wrote:

"Doctor George Hodel, M.D. 5121 Fountain [Franklin] Avenue, at the time of this murder had a clinic at East First Street near Alameda. Lillian DeNorak [Lenorak] who lived with this doctor said he spent some time around the Biltmore Hotel and identified the photo of victim Short as a photo of one of the doctor's girlfriends. Tamar Hodel, 15-year-old daughter, stated that her mother, Dorothy Hodel, has told her that her father had been out all night on a party the night of the murder and said, 'They'll never be able to prove I did that murder.' Two microphones were placed in this suspect's home, which tend to prove his innocence.... Rudolph Walthers, known to have been acquainted with victim and also with suspect Hodel, claimed he had not seen victim in the presence of Hodel and did not believe that the doctor had ever met the victim."

Jemison included a list of acquaintances, none of which could connect Hodel to Short. In fact, Detective Brian Carr, the LAPD officer in charge of the Black Dahlia case at the time of Steve Hodel's briefing said, that if he ever took a case as weak as Hodel's to a prosecutor, he'd be "laughed out of the office."

In yet another book, Hodel claims his father is also the infamous Zodiac Killer. This raises serious issues with his credibility. It seems as if he's looking for a way to generate book sales by associating his father with the most high profile cases. This is like ghost hunters or mediums that report only celebrity ghosts.

Forensically, facial recognition software could possibly clear this up, but despite Holdel's law enforcement experience, he didn't use this resource. We consider this a red flag. Hodel cannot just say that his father's photos resemble Short, because his picture collection could be compared to existing photos of Elizabeth Short.

Tunnel Vision

The primary complication in Black Dahlia murder theories is that the evidence is ambiguous and each person who writes about the case seems to have some personal agenda toward which he molds whatever evidence there is.

Criminologist Kim Rossmo has made a study of how cognitive errors specifically affect investigations. He discusses how investigators arrive at scenes with a perceptual set. These mindsets help them decide what to do next, but they can become problematic if the decisions are premature or too entrenched in a specific idea (threshold diagnosis). People tend to see what they expect to see (confirmation bias). Recall of events is more consistent with personal beliefs than with facts, especially as it supports someone's formulated hypothesis (due to either confirmation bias or belief perseverance), and contradictory information is generally ignored. That's just the way our minds work.

Rossmo points out that clear and rational thinking is not automatic and "our brains are not wired to deal effectively with uncertainty." To organize information for daily use, we rely on mental shortcuts called heuristics. For example, the anchoring heuristic is the tendency to remain with our starting point, ignoring or failing to perceive anything that might alter it.

"Tunnel vision results when there is a narrow focus on a limited range of alternatives," Rossmo states. Problems with evidence result from hasty, incomplete, or biased interpretation, and can get muddled in memory from misinformation (whether from witnesses or other investigators). The result of these pressures can be a quick threshold diagnosis, which limits the focus and potentially ignores good leads.

The formation of a perceptual set involves two primary avenues for processing information. Some information goes through rational channels and some through emotional or intuitive channels. Intuition is aligned with automatic, subconscious judgment and highly influenced by emotion. It is fast and its conclusions are made without analysis. Thus, it is vulnerable to error.

Although reasoning is slower, it offers awareness of a greater range of factors, and the result of careful analysis is usually more reliable. In other words, what *feels* right is not necessarily right. Gut instinct often results in a threshold diagnosis that can become an immovable anchor.

After twenty-three years of working with various mediums ("psychics," or "sensitives") Mark has seen numerous instances where their results are *less* prone to the various bias's crime scene investigators are. "Obviously, if a psychic is investigating on a battlefield, it would be easy for them to come up with information they say they're receiving from a soldier—an example of confirmation bias. But just as often they contact a spirit that has nothing to do with the most important history of the site—the battle. They will contact, perhaps, a civilian of an earlier or later time period than the significant era associated with a site. It might turn out that it was the original owner of the site—sometimes Native Americans—or individuals who may have died recently in a house."

What is unusual is that, when they do contact a soldier from a battle they often name the state the soldier came from and that information aligns with the historical records.

As well, other than empaths who may feel the emotion of a traumatic incident from the past, they seem rather unemotional about the information they're receiving. They may be surprised or sometimes shocked by what comes to them, but no more shocked than a non-sensitive person reading a newspaper or watching TV.

Paranormal investigators, as opposed to psychics, however, seem more inclined towards confirmation bias. In gathering EVP for example, they assume that the voice on the recorder is that of the spirit they're addressing. Often a disembodied voice on the recorder will not answer the question asked or make some other non-sensical response, indicating the spirit is of someone other than whom the investigators are querying. Caution must be made not to assume anything in paranormal investigating until it can be confirmed by a secondary source.

Investigative Logic

Officer John St. John took charge of the Black Dahlia case in the 1960s. An author, John Gilmore, approached him with a tape recording that he said was given to him by a tall, thin man, who walked with a limp and had a long rap sheet for robbery and sexual offenses. This man went by the name of Arnold Smith and he claimed that a character named Al Morrison had confessed to killing Elizabeth Short. In fact, they'd been together on the night it occurred. Smith showed Gilmore a box of Short's belongings, including a handkerchief and a photo of her with Smith, a blond woman, and 'Morrison.' Smith said that he'd taken Short to a room in a Hollywood hotel, along with Morrison. Short had been surprised that Morrison was planning to stay in the room, too, and refused to drink with him.

She was uninterested in a fling, so Morrison took her to a house on East 31st Street, where they had a physical fight. Morrison knocked her out and got a paring knife, butcher knife and some clothesline. He tied her up. When Short revived, he stuffed her panties into her mouth. He then stabbed her numerous times until she expired. To drain her body of blood, he took it to the bathtub and cut it in half. He washed everything clean, performed a few mutilations, and finally took it out and placed the pieces in the vacant lot.

Unfortunately, before this tale could be corroborated, Smith set his room on fire and burned to death. If he actually had the photos or effects of Short's that he claimed to have, these, too, were destroyed. Perhaps Short's ghost keeps showing up because nothing has yet been resolved.

The Coed Killer

Katherine grew up in Ann Arbor, Michigan, where a serial killer was active when she was a kid. At the time, he'd been so elusive that some people believed he had paranormal powers. They called him the Devil. Once, while cops were inside investigating a site, it seemed that he (or someone) had left lilac blossoms outside, one for each victim—in broad daylight! There were seven victims in the area, and the person finally convicted for the last murder but implicitly attached to the others was 20-year-old John Norman Collins. Every bit the handsome and charming all-American boy that Ted Bundy was, he had plans to become an elementary school teacher.

All of this occurred during a time when few people really understood the concept of a serial killer. The Boston Strangler had been active a few years before, but the idea of a man randomly killing young women in a prominent college town was unnerving. However, it was the end of the sixties and race riots had rocked nearby Detroit. Then a young woman—the first victim—-turned up missing.

On Tuesday, August 8, 1967, the *Ann Arbor News* described the first of the so-called coed murders: "A body found yesterday afternoon on a Superior Township farm was tentatively identified as that of a 19-year-old Eastern Michigan University coed who disappeared without a trace July 9."

The body turned out to be that of Mary Fleszar. She was last seen by a roommate leaving their apartment near campus to go for a walk. She was five-foot-two, weighed about 110 pounds, wore glasses, and had brown hair.

Two teenage boys that Katherine knew back then found her body. They were preparing to plow a field when they heard a car door slam. Thinking they might witness a pair of lovers, they sneaked closer to the foundation of the former farmhouse, a sort of dumping site and lovers' lane combined. The car door slammed again and an engine turned over, but by the time they reached the area, the car was gone. They noticed fresh tire tracks in the weeds and followed them to a spot where they noticed a putrid odor. Then they spotted a blackish-brown form with leathery skin, which they thought was a dead deer. Flies crawled all over it in the summer heat. The carcass appeared to have a head, but it was rotten and shapeless. Then one of them noticed that the ear looked human, so they ran to get the police.

The responding officers immediately recognized the body as human. It was nude, lying on its side, facedown. One forearm and hand and the fingers of the other hand were missing. Both feet were severed at the ankles, and the skin showed animal bites. The medical examiner estimated that the victim had been dead at least a month, and she was quickly identified as the missing coed. The autopsy found evidence that she'd been stabbed in the chest thirty times. Detectives who examined the crime scene said the body had been moved at least three times. It was first placed on top of a pile of bottles and cans, and then moved five feet south. Later, it was moved three more feet. Clearly, whoever was out there the day the boys heard a car door slam was there to see her.

The next body would not be discovered for a year, but over the next thirteen months after that, five would be found in roughly the same area. Then they began to turn up much more quickly.

Many years later, Katherine returned to where the first victim had lain for those two months to see if she could get any interesting photos or EVPs. Stories had popped up that the figure of a young woman was sometimes seen out there. On the way, Katherine passed by where the youngest victim, a 13-year-old, had been tossed on the roadside. Only a few more miles and she would reach the cemetery where another one had been shot in the head (by someone else, as it turned out). That incident, too, had produced a ghost, but this was no surprise, since it was quite near Denton Road, where ghost tales were abundant.

Once at the scene, Katherine noted that the temperature had dropped considerably in the past hour and was now in the thirties. Darkness was closing in. In order to get close to the site, she climbed over a pipe and walked through prickly weeds to the foundation of the old farmhouse. She walked the property's perimeter and took photos. The place was still as trashy as it had been back when the police had sifted through the garbage for clues and found the victim's orange dress. She sensed that she'd get the best results at the old foundation, so she snapped several from different angles.

Then she tried EVP, but it was windy and the sound of cars from the nearby road kept intruding. Later, she saw that she got a few orbs in the photos, but nothing dramatic. She did hear that ghost stories had popped up in other places.

One rumor holds that if you drive past the area where several victims were found in a farmhouse foundation (a different one), the trunk of your car will pop open. You can still see the silo where the farm used to be, which is supposedly haunted by the girl murdered there.

Another scene is much closer to the Eastern Michigan University campus. While Collins attended EMU, he lived and may have committed some crimes at 619 Emmet St., which is now home to the Alpha Xi Delta sorority house. Supposedly, people hear voices and doors closing randomly at the house on Emmet, although no one is around. Collins is still alive, in prison, so it's not *his* ghost.

A Killer's Cemetery

Serial killers don't often commit suicide, but one who did left behind a large property where he'd buried many bodies. People today claim that Fox Hollow Farm in Westfield, once owned by Herb Baumeister, is quite haunted. It's been the subject of several paranormal investigations.

Fox Hollow Farm

Nearly a dozen young men went missing between 1993 and 1995. Some of their faces were put on posters, asking the public for help. A tipster told police about a regular patron at the gay bars who invited young men to his home for "dangerous" sex. This man, who went by the name "Brian Smart," had called the tipster several times and hinted at having "bad nights." The tipster believed the man had killed a friend of his. Police told him to let them know if he spotted "Brian Smart" again. He saw him in 1996 and took down his license plate number, which he turned over to the police. The person of interest was Baumeister.

Apparently, he was living a double life. He had a wife, family, and prosperous business. They lived quite well. Nevertheless, officers questioned Baumeister and asked to search his home. He refused. They did a search of his eighteen-acre estate by air with infrared technology. If there were graves on the property, this was one way of locating them. However, the search produced nothing.

Baumeister's wife, Julie, learned about the police interest in him and she, too, refused to let them search. But she was stunned by the possibility that her husband might be having sex with males. Worse, he might be killing them. She knew that he'd once spent two months in a psychiatric institution, but this had been twenty years earlier. Still, she knew that he'd had opportunities when she'd been on trips, not to mention the numerous business trips that he took, and lately he'd been having terrible mood swings. Things grew tense between them, the business floundered, and Julie filed for divorce in order to keep custody of their children. She was now afraid of her husband. In 1996, Julie Baumeister gave investigators permission to search the property.

Baumeister fled to Ontario, Canada. He knew what they would find. It wasn't long before they dug up evidence of dead bodies. Right away, it looked like they had at least seven victims here on the property, possibly more. They kept excavating.

In a park in Grand Bend on July 3, 1996, Baumeister sat on the shore of a lake and shot himself in the forehead with a .357 Magnum revolver. He left a 3-page note. He regretted messing up the park, he wrote, and felt badly about his broken marriage and failing business, but he did not admit to any crime.

From over 5,000 bone fragments and teeth, police confirmed the remains of eleven victims and suspected Baumeister in the murders of at least nine others, a string attributed to the "I-70 Killer," who was never identified. I-70 was Baumeister's business route.

After Baumeister's suicide, Julie took the kids and left. The mansion stood empty for years. Finally, a couple purchased the farm and gutted the mansion. They experienced odd things, like knocking on doors when no one was there, and saw a man in a red T-shirt who'd disappeared in front of them. He'd had no legs. There was also an image of a man seemingly running for his life. Several paranormal groups have investigated the place, getting EVPs and images on cameras. They believe the hauntings are centered in the poolroom in the basement where Baumeister killed many of his victims.

One man who rented an apartment on the property claims to have seen and recorded the voice of Baumeister himself. Supposedly, the voice said, "the married one," although as an identification of the infamous serial killer, it's not what we'd call evidence.

The Murder House

Villisca, Iowa, was a small but flourishing town along the railway during the early 1900s – in contrast to its isolated existence today. Once popular and busy, it's now described as somewhat forlorn. In 1912, Villisca's residents numbered about 2500, according to several official sources, so when an unexpected massacre occurred on June 10, it became a major news story. We described this place in

Blood & Ghosts, but we want to say more about the investigation here.

Mary Peckham, a neighbor of the J. B. Moore family, realized that no one was up and about as usual on Monday, June 10. She went to see if everything was okay, but clearly, it wasn't. She fetched J. B.'s brother, Ross Moore.

After checking around, Ross came to the house. He went around to a bedroom window to see if he could find someone inside to let him in, but the curtains were closed. He rapped and listened, but got no response. Next, he tried the doors. Front and back were both locked, which was uncharacteristic. Since he had his own key, he let himself in.

There were three rooms on the ground floor: a parlor, a kitchen and a bedroom. Ross called out to J. B. and then Sarah, and finally steeled himself to walk through the kitchen. There was no sign that a meal had been prepared that day, although a plate sat out in the open. Crossing the dark and silent parlor, he opened the door to the bedroom. He was there but a moment before he rushed back and shouted for Mary to get the sheriff. He'd seen enough blood to realize that someone had been murdered.

John Henry "Hank" Horton arrived. Although just a peace officer, Horton knew what death smelled like. As he went into the first-floor bedroom, he saw that the white sheets were heavily stained with blood. Against the wall rested a long-handled ax with dark stains on it, and Horton noted one more odd detail: Dark material that appeared to be torn clothing covered the mirror.

He then climbed the stairs. The smell of death reached his nostrils again from the stuffy second floor, so he guessed at what he was in for.

At the top of the steps was a bedroom. Horton entered and saw a sight similar to what he'd encountered downstairs—sheet-covered forms and bloody walls. Opening a curtain to let in some light, he looked around. J.

B. and Sarah Moore had both received smashing blows to their skulls as they slept.

In the next bedroom, which held three beds, Horton raised the shade and saw four dead children in this room, two of them in one bed. Blood covered all of the bedclothes and stained the walls—even the ceiling. He realized now that everyone in this family was dead, their heads crushed in.

But the Moores had just four children and he had eight bodies, so who were the two downstairs? He had to go back down to try to identify them and alert their parents.

Horton realized he had a case that would make headlines around the country. Mass deaths, such as what had just happened on April 14 with the sinking of the Titanic and the loss of more than 1500 lives, were always big news. Ax murders were not uncommon, since it was one of the few lethal implements that could be used silently, but the slaughter of an entire family was certainly rare—eight all at once! How had this perpetrator subdued them all? And what could be his motive for such a bloody deed?

The Moores were an affluent family with a wide circle of acquaintances and associates. The phone operators who overheard the early phone calls passed along a few details themselves to their own acquaintances. That's how the Stillingers learned that their daughters, Lena, 12, and Ina, 8, were among the dead. The girls had been allowed to spend the night at the Moore's home after the children's program at the church.

Dr. Cooper accompanied Horton to the house as fast as he could. He knew from Horton that bloodhounds, some county officials, and a private detective were on the way, but for the moment, the onus of identification was on them.

However, it was not just these two men who entered the home, but with them were Dr. W. A. Lomas, Dr. F. S.

Williams, and the Reverend Ewing—far too many to take care to preserve the evidence.

The skulls and faces of the victims were so smashed into bone, hair and brain matter that no one in the party recognized who they were. The younger girl, approximately 7 or 8, lay nearest the wall, and seemed relatively undisturbed. The physicians agreed that she'd likely died from the first blow, and the others had been delivered after, possibly to ensure her death.

The other child in that room appeared to have been molested, or at least sexually posed. Her nightgown was up and she wore no underwear. One arm was over her head, under the pillow, and one leg was splayed outward. She appeared to have been turned over slightly to the right after she'd been bludgeoned, as the line of blood had dripped onto the bed before her hand had gone into that position. Her right knee bore a bloodstain as well, though there were no wounds to her legs or lower torso. Perhaps she'd felt the blow, struggled, and was dispatched only after she'd been hit again. These were Lena and Ina Stillinger.

The person who had suffered the most was J. B. He'd apparently been struck repeatedly, in a form of overkill that indicated either rage or fear that the only adult male in the house could not be easily dispatched. J. B. was on his back, with his left hand lying over his chest. His face had been cut so often the eyes were gone. The way he'd been brutalized would inspire speculation about enemies he may have had, business rivals, or disgruntled employees.

As for the children, on one cot lay a boy on his stomach, who'd taken the fierce blows to the back of his skull. The killer had then placed a gauze undershirt over the open wound, as if to soak up the blood. Not far from this victim was a little girl, her face bashed in and a blood-spattered dress lying partly on her head. The sheet was pulled up over her head as well.

Finally, on a single bed, two murdered boys lay together. According to the official report delivered by one of the doctors at the scene, both of the tops of their heads were beaten in, and blood lay all over the pillows. It appeared as if they'd died instantly. The coroner noted that it seemed as if the brains of all the children had been "chopped out by some instrument." He thought, as stated in one source, that each person had been struck between twenty and thirty times, and over J. B.'s head, a gouge mark indicated the killer had raised the ax fairly high for at least one blow. (This number is likely an over-estimate or exaggeration, or erroneously reported, as the total number of blows that night would have been well over one hundred fifty, and the heads would probably have been nothing but pulp.)

Villisca House

The coroner found a piece of a keychain and a four-pound slab of raw bacon (some sources say two pounds), wrapped in a cloth and lying on the floor in the downstairs bedroom near the ax. Another piece, nearly the same size, was in the icebox in the kitchen, where both the inside and outside doors had been locked. On a table stood a bowl containing bloody water and a plate of food, prepared but not consumed.

The only other potential pieces of physical evidence were the ripped clothing covering a glass and several mirrors, the glass chimney of a lamp lying under a dresser, and a heel mark on a magazine lying on a closet floor. Also, Sarah's blood-filled shoe was on J. B.'s side of the bed, as if picked up and moved. Dr. Linquist assumed that blood had pooled and dripped into it from J. B's head wound, and it was then tipped over. The ax, too, had been wiped off, as there were cloth fibers on it, and the killer had cleaned off his hands on several items.

There were also items in the barn. There was a depression in some hay that was about the size and shape of a man who might have been lying in it. To Lindquist's mind, it looked recent. In fact, it appeared that a two-inch knothole had been utilized as a way to spy, because it was near where the shape of a head had been and it afforded a view of the rear of the house.

Sheriff Oren Jackson arrived to help Horton make sense of the scene, aware that the killer had a head start, but not much of one.

The bloodhound handler arrived late that evening with the pair of dogs from Beatrice, Nebraska, but so many people had been in the house and handled items like the suspected murder weapon that it was probably impossible for the hounds to get a scent. They did sniff with interest along a trail that led through town to the nearby river, but they lost it there and couldn't pick anything up on the other side. It seemed the killer, if that's whom they were following, had decided to walk through the water, getting out who-knows-where.

J. B. and his wife Sarah were well liked in the community, active in their church, and helpful to neighbors. They'd been married since 1899 and had four children, ages 5 to 11, three boys and a girl. Sarah had coordinated the Children's Day Program at church, which had run until 9:30 on Sunday evening, at which time she and J. B. had gathered their children and the Stillinger girls. They had walked home, laughing and waving to acquaintances as they went.

Some time between midnight and five o'clock in the morning, the slaughter occurred. The ax had belonged to J. B., so whoever had grabbed it had been in one of the outbuildings. Although bloody, the killer had made some effort to clean it before leaning it against the wall where it was found.

Apparently this grim reaper had lighted his way, but just barely, with a kerosene lamp, found at the foot of the bed where J. B. and Sarah had been killed. Its glass chimney had been removed and placed under a dresser. Another such lamp was in the ground floor bedroom, also with the wick turned down.

Yet, he had to have made a considerable amount of noise as he cracked skulls and jabbed the ax into ceilings, as well as when climbing the stairs. It was a mystery how he could have gone about his business, waking no one. It seemed that, except for Lena, they all lay still, killed in their sleep.

Since he'd covered most of the victim's heads or faces, there was reason to believe that he might have been acquainted with them, or that he believed if they opened their eyes and saw him, his visage might be impressed in the retina and thus detectable at autopsy – a common superstition of the day. He then drew the curtains, possibly after he'd disabled everyone and before he went back to use the ax blade on them all, or possibly when it was all over (although they did not have blood on them). Those windows without curtains he blacked out with clothing found inside the house. An unexplained piece of this puzzle was the skirt he had torn and draped over several mirrors. Perhaps it was a ritual, perhaps a reflex, perhaps superstition.

In some cultures, mirrors were covered during sleep or illness so that the soul, which might wander, would not become trapped. After a death, mirrors were also covered or turned to face the wall as a way to prevent the deceased's soul from becoming caught in the mirror, delaying its journey to the afterlife, as well as to prevent the living from having their souls trapped in the mirror when in the presence of the dead.

Given the degree of overkill evident in this crime, an obvious suspect would have been someone holding a grudge. This seemed to describe a business rival, Frank Jones, for whom J.B. had worked for nine years. After a bitter parting, J.B. had started his own implements store, luring away some of Jones's larger customers, including the John Deere Plow franchise. Jones had become a politician and had served in the House of Representatives and state Senate; he'd also founded the Villisca National Bank. Thus, he was in a position of prestige and control, and some citizens described him as arrogant. In addition to his possible anger over the professional betrayal, there were rumors that J.B. had had an affair with Jones's daughter-in-law.

Jones might not have committed the murders himself, but with his considerable wealth, he could have hired someone. Jones denied having anything to do with it.

Given the potential that the killer had been watching the house from a hiding spot, such behavior seemed less that of a successful businessman and more that of a stalker. Perhaps someone had been in love from afar, in a perverted way, with Sarah, and had finally been unable to control the urge to kill those she loved, along with her.

There were many rumors about the culprit's identity, including information viewed in tealeaves and the vision offered by Mrs. Hamilton, a self-proclaimed psychic in a nearby town. She "saw" a large man with a dark mustache and a hat. She said he'd turn himself in and also indicated, erroneously, that the murder weapon was near another building.

More interesting was a mentally unstable preacher who became obsessed with the killings and supposedly confessed, but this happened later. In addition, over the years, men who appeared to be serial killers have been offered as suspects. Indeed, there was a documented trail of ax murders at that time across the Midwest. Just nine months earlier, there had been several ax murders nearly seven hundred miles away in Colorado Springs, Colorado.

The first had also occurred on a Sunday night—September 17, 1911—and three people died in the home of H. C. Wayne. Apparently, that was not enough for this fiend, because the family next door suffered the same fate as they slept. The killer entered the home of Mrs. A. J. Burns who had two children, and all were slaughtered with an ax. All six victims had suffered ax blows to the head.

Two weeks later, in Monmouth, Illinois, an intruder took what appeared to be an ax to William Dawson and his wife and daughter. Then in Kansas, on October 15 and June 5—this one just a week before Villisca—two more families met an untimely fate. In Ellsworth, there were five victims: the entire William Showman family, while in Paola, Roland Hudson and his wife were bludgeoned. The pick-ax used had been left behind in another building.

Some analysts said that the crimes had key similarities, such as the MO and time of the crime, which pointed to a single killer, while others said that they had key differences.

Commentators today indicate that the concept of a serial killer was not well known, so linkage analysis was not yet developed. In fact, America had been through a number of cases of serial murder.

Belle Gunness killed and buried over a dozen men on her pig farm. H. H. Holmes, in Chicago, had been suspected in more than 100 murders. In Austin, Texas, in 1885, the Servant Girl Annihilator had murdered 5 women in the course of a year. On Joseph Briggen's California ranch, also a pig enterprise, the bones of 12 men had been found. In addition, numerous poisoners had killed a string of victims, and there were several series of unsolved murders in at least 5 states, aside from those under consideration for association with Villisca.

Three months after the Villisca slaughter, back in Quincy, Illinois, Charles Pfanschmidt, his wife, daughter, and guest were murdered. The house was set on fire, but the bodies were discovered and it was clear that they'd been killed in their sleep with an ax. Although it appeared that the son of the couple, living elsewhere, was the culprit, rumors abounded that this incident was another that should be attributed to the Midwest ax killer. Still, the son was convicted.

In December 1912, six months after the Villisca event, Henry Moore (no relation) was arrested, prosecuted, and convicted of the ax murders of his wife and maternal grandmother in Columbia, Missouri. Moore had been an ornery drifter, prone to episodes of anger, so he might be considered a suspect in the Iowa massacre. Indeed, by some accounts, he'd spent a year in Leavenworth for a petty crime; since his fingerprints were on file, he might know to wear gloves in any future crimes.

The man whom Frank Jones had supposedly hired to commit the crime, William Mansfield, was associated with another episode of killing with an ax. Two years after the

Moores were killed in their beds, Mansfield became a suspect in the ax murders of members of his own family—his wife, child and in-laws.

In many of the homes, the mirrors had been covered. In one or two, the chimney of a lamp had been removed, like in the Moore home. In one place, a washbasin was filled with bloody water.

The Reverend Lyn George J. Kelly, at just over 5 feet and weighing about 115 pounds, was a scrawny and excitable traveling preacher from Macedonia, Iowa, not far from Villisca. He'd come into town on Saturday, June 8, and the following day had been in attendance at the church where the Moore family and Stillinger girls had participated in the children's program. Yet it was clear to those who encountered him that he disliked children and was exceedingly agitated, often speaking too fast to be understood. He left town early the following morning, which made him a prime suspect (though he was scheduled to leave), but he exacerbated the situation considerably in 1917 by confessing. In addition, there was testimony that Kelly had told some people on the train on the morning of the murders that 8 people had been killed in Villisca. That statement had occurred prior to 7:00 A.M., before bodies were discovered.

In a letter penned by Lena Atkinson, who'd had exposure as a child to Kelly on the evening before the murders, she said, "We youngsters always heard the minister had confessed the crime on the train going to Macedonia. As we heard it, he had received a vision to follow the biblical injunction, 'Slay and slay utterly.' Whether that is in the Bible I have no idea, but we as youngsters always repeated it to each other.... I do remember my parents always believed Rev. Kelly committed the Villisca Ax Murders."

In addition, Kelly wrote letters to the authorities about the murders and seems to have sent a bloodstained shirt to be laundered. This item was never recovered for evidence. In his town, Kelly was known as a Peeping Tom.

In his confession, Kelly said that on the night of June 9, he'd heard the sound of windmills and went for a walk to clear his head. He was pondering a sermon about "slaying utterly," and he found himself in front of the Moore house. In a trancelike state, he found the ax, went inside, and started to kill. He claimed he killed the adults first, and then he heard a voice to keep going, so he bludgeoned the Moore children. Ending in the downstairs bedroom, he heard God's voice again, so he then finished off the Stillinger girls.

From a crime scene analysis, authorities believed the killer was left-handed, so to get some evidence after his confession, they asked Kelly to chop some wood. He obliged, swinging it left-handed. It seemed to many involved in the case that they'd found the killer at last.

However, before the trial, Kelly recanted his confession, and his attorney, W. E. Mitchell, would dismiss it in court as the result of an intense inquisition that had lasted a full night, undertaken to "shield" someone else (a statement suggestive of political connections). He claimed that after the ordeal, "Kelly was more dead than alive, more insane than sane."

Kelly's trial began in September 1917. The challenge for his defense team was to prove that Kelly was of unsound mind and had perhaps developed such an obsession with the Villisca incident that he'd come to have delusions about himself as the killer. Apparently, he'd been known to ramble on and on about the murders, having developed this obsession after getting a tour of the home late in June 1912. At that time, he'd imagined himself a detective and had claimed he'd received training at Scotland Yard. He also proved to be a habitual false confessor. There was no physical evidence that actually tied Kelly to the murders.

The result was a hung jury: they couldn't come to an agreement. Eleven men wanted to acquit Kelly and one wanted to find him not guilty by reason of insanity. He was tried a second time in November, and this time he was acquitted.

Over the one hundred-plus year span since the Moore-Stillinger murders, the murder house has gone through at least eight different owners. Some rented out the building, and it deteriorated over the years, until 1994, when Darwin and Martha Linn purchased and renovated the place to resemble how it had looked on the fateful morning of June 10, 1912. They already ran the Olson-Linn Museum, so they had a clear interest in local history. The original furniture was long gone, so the Linns purchased antiques to provide a semblance of the place from long ago.

Now on the National Register of Historic Places, the J. B. Moore house is open for tours. Called the Villisca Ax Murder House, it draws many people interested not only in history or crime but also in the paranormal. One can pay for an overnight tour—with the hope of having "an experience." Supposedly children's voices or banging sounds have been heard. Someone reported falling objects, while several visitors have felt the presence of someone who can't be seen. Oil lamps blow out, although there's no breeze, and many people claim to have photographic evidence of something that hovers in the air.

The tours start at the Olson Linn museum on the Town Square.

Ghost hunter Troy Taylor went to experience the house for himself in May 2005. He scheduled an overnight investigation for a group, including it in *So, There I Was.* First, they went to the cemetery where the victims had been buried, the monuments for which had been purchased from reward money that was never paid out.

Inside the house, Taylor noted that it lacked electricity and plumbing, and described his awareness of the echoes of the successive murders. Appropriately for ghost hunting, a thunderstorm gathered in the distance. One of the people hoping to see or hear a ghost had brought along candy as enticement for a child.

A camera was set up in the children's bedroom, with a video feed to the kitchen. That night, everyone involved witnessed a phenomenon: when candy was offered in exchange for closing a specified door, the door would close on its own.

"It did not slam closed," Taylor writes, "but rather seemed to just gently close, as though someone was pushing it. There was absolutely no one near it at this time."

Taylor examined it for wires, a draft, a slope to the house, and any other natural or manipulated explanation. They left it standing for two hours without the sugary inducement and it did not close. Then they offered candy once again. The door closed and latched.

Taylor took this as pretty fair proof that the place was haunted—or at least, that some force had been disturbed by the recent renovations. He tried everything he could think of to prove that the closing door had a reasonable explanation, but came up empty-handed.

Lizzie Borden Revisited

We included the Lizzie Borden house in *Blood & Ghosts*, but another investigation was undertaken for the television series *Monster Quest*, which aired in August 2013. Katherine had once interviewed the voice analyst they used on the show, Tom Owen, so we're including his response to the EVP collected.

To review, Katherine had collected documents and analyzed the double homicide in Fall River, MA, 1892, for former FBI profiler, John Douglas. While there, she did some ghost recordings, so she was able to examine this case from a variety of investigative angles.

Briefly, here's what happened: On August 4, 1892, Andrew Borden, age 70, and his wife Abby, age 65, were murdered in their home. Andrew's corpse was discovered in a semi-reclining position on the living-room couch, his battered head resting on his rolled-up coat and his face cut open. There were blood spatters on the floor around him, up the wall, and on the picture hanging over the sofa, but oddly, Borden's clothing was undisturbed. It appeared as though he was napping, except one eye, sliced in half, was staring at the ceiling. It appeared that someone standing over him had attacked him from above. When he came home that morning, he was unaware that his wife, Abby, lay dead in the guest room upstairs.

Borden's adult daughter, Lizzie, found his corpse. She was thirty-two and, as a single woman, was living at home. The only other person in the house that morning was the live-in maid, Bridget Sullivan. Lizzie's sister Emma and Uncle John were out visiting. A neighbor went looking for Abby and found her upstairs in the guest bedroom. Abby Borden, lying facedown, had been hit multiple times with a sharp weapon, possibly a hatchet. It soon became clear that she'd been killed over an hour before Andrew.

Lizzie became the prime suspect and went through a sensational trial, but was acquitted. Within six months, she had sold the murder house at 92 Second Street with most of the furnishings, using her considerable inheritance to purchase a mansion in the wealthy area of town. She was buried in the family plot with her murdered parents and her sister, Emma, from whom she'd become estranged.

Lizzie Borden House

Through the years, as the house changed hands, there were reports of ghostly occurrences. Katherine had picked up some EVP, and another crew had experienced a camera shifting by itself about 45 degrees. The new owner as of 2004 said that she stayed in the maid's room one night. When she awoke, she saw that a small rocking chair that had been to the left of the bed was now next to her, as if someone had been watching her. There were also tales about the ghostly figure of an elderly woman in the guest room and an old-fashioned sewing machine in the corner that reportedly started up on its own. A few guests had seen the impressions of heads on the pillows, and one had taken a photo that showed shadowy figures in a window.

In *Blood & Ghosts*, we provided our own approach to an investigation here, and *Monster Quest* pretty much duplicated this, but without a psychic. They also added a professional forensic voice analyst.

Let us say a few things about the show first. The purported approach is to use scientists to analyze photos, audios, and videos. In one instance, the supposed photo of a ghost in the Vatican was quickly and easily debunked. However, videos of what appeared to be a dust fragment on a lens and of several soldiers walking through the infamous Triangular Field at Gettysburg were hardly subjected to a thorough analysis. Both analysts admitted they couldn't rule out the paranormal, but neither had actually used a scientific method. Despite their credentials, their efforts for the show were underwhelming. This signaled that the show wasn't really attempting to clarify anything about the paranormal, not in a serious way.

To see if the video of the soldiers was faked (because some moving images of the backs of men exactly duplicated others), they should have used a forgery detection algorithm, like we mentioned earlier.

Yet we're primarily concerned here with the Lizzie Borden house. During a 50-hour overnight investigation for the show, not much happened except that a FLIR (forward-looking infrared) camera picked up a hot spot underneath a toy chest that no one could explain and there were two EVPs. Both "voices" were given to Tom Owen. One supposedly said "Sure" and the other was a breathy "Sooo."

Audio forensics depends on a mix of high-tech software and human interpretation. An audio examiner's job involves enhancing tapes to make them easier to hear, checking them for tampering, and identifying (if possible) the people speaking. Ideally, the recording should be at least seven seconds long. The software does a spectrograph analysis, an average pitch analysis, and a statistical analysis involving a database. The match quality (if one is trying to match to a source) should be at least 60%, based on comparing the accent, syntax and breathing patterns.

In Europe, analysts have access to a database of constant electronic network frequency activity from power companies, which makes it possible to determine on some tapes with a background hum the day and time a recording was made. This is not yet available in the U.S.

Tom Owen, a reputable forensic analyst, said on *Monster Quest* that he'd be able to tell by pitch and other characteristics whether a voice was human. When Katherine interviewed him, Owen ran Owl Investigations, Inc, which offered his service as a certified Voice Identification Examiner.

Owen consults with law enforcement agencies and has served as an expert witness. His processing laboratory had several different types of spectrograph machines, and he attests to their forensic utility. For example, Owen analyzed the scream on the 911 tape that was at the center of the George Zimmerman trial.

"It's not uncommon," Owen said to Katherine, "that at a murder scene or shooting, you have a tape made from a 911 call where the victim might have been calling for help, or else they might have been on the phone talking to a relative. Someone shoots them, they die and the shooter doesn't realize that the machine was recording. I would get that tape and see if the intruder said anything before they shot the person. Sometimes we get results. Then there are civil incidents, like someone calling to threaten you."

He'd performed a study on twenty-five female voices of varying races and ages, doing a one-to-one analysis to determine the degree of error. The results were striking: "When you're comparing a known and an unknown voice using a verbatim exemplar [the samples contain the same verbal communication], there are no errors. That's ninety-nine percent of what we do today. We don't try to pick a voice out of a pack."

Yet, because of error rates among interpreters, this technology is not always accepted in court. Even so, it can contribute to an investigation.

How? The vocal column begins in the vocal folds and ends at the lips. The vocal folds provide a closed end so that the vocal column becomes a resonator, with vocal fold tension determining the frequency of the vibrations. When a sound is produced, those harmonics nearest the vocal column's resonant frequency increase in amplitude.

The spectrograph converts the voice into a visual graphic display, the voiceprint. With an analog spectrograph, a magnetic high-quality tape is fastened to a scanning drum, which holds a measured segment of tape time. The process takes about eighty to ninety seconds to complete. As the drum revolves, an electronic filter starts up and acts as a gatekeeper: It allows only a certain band of frequencies to get through. They're translated into electrical energy that gets written by a stylus onto special paper. As the process continues, the filter moves into increasingly higher frequencies and the stylus records the intensity levels of each defined range. The final print shows a pattern of closely spaced lines that represent 2.5 seconds worth of all of the distinguishable frequencies of the target person's taped voice.

The horizontal axis on a voiceprint registers how high or low a voice is. The vertical axis is the frequency. The degree of darkness within each region on the graph illustrates intensity or volume. These prints can be filed into a computer after being coded, or can be produced as a bar print, which is useful for identification.

For accurate identification, voiceprint analysts use two methods:

1. Aural: listening to the known and questioned samples to compare single sounds and series of sounds, and to listen for breath patterns,

inflections, unusual speech habits, and accents.

2. Visual: reading the voiceprints on the graph.

The highest standard for court requires the identification of twenty distinct speech sounds that possess similarities. Audio enhancement may involve noise reduction, or the attempt to restore or heighten nearly inaudible sounds. Technicians apply compression, equalization and an increase in amplitude. Intelligibility requires more complex engineering. It may involve zeroing in on a specific region of the tape or selective elimination— removing one sound to enhance another. The desired signal can be separated as long as it doesn't share the same frequency as the one to be eliminated.

Owen placed the recordings through his devices, despite the fact that neither came close to being seven seconds in duration. The first one, "Sure" did not show up as a genuine voice, despite sounding very much like a female voice. However, the second one, "Sooo," which sounded quite close to the microphone, although cameras showed that no one was near the recorder, was more interesting to him. Owen said that it manifested like a voice, but he did not definitively accept that it was a paranormal voice. Still, the show left this up in the air, as if attempting to appease both sides by taking no side.

While engaging the efforts of a voice analysis expert has potential, bear in mind that information obtained via a paranormal investigation is different. EVP, remember, is *"electronic* voice phenomena." It is created without the same physical mechanisms—palate, tongue, teeth, lips, larynx, and throat—as regular speech and may not exhibit the same characteristics. EVP shows up on magnetic recording tape and computer chips within a digital recorder without any accompanying audible sound waves. It may or may not produce the same visual graphic in a studio that regular sound makes, yet words, to human ears, are often recognizable.

The museum today has set up a series of "ghost cams" to which one can subscribe as part of a "community." According to the website, "all the cameras are 720 DPI High Def, High Gain sound with night vision." There is one in each primary bedroom (running only when the room is not booked), and a live 24/7 camera in the basement.

The Hotel Chelsea

The Hotel Chelsea is at 222 West 23rd Street, in the New York City area of art galleries and flea markets known as Chelsea. This eleven-story building went up in 1884 as a residential co-op. The hotel's reputation as a "cauldron for creativity" came from the numerous artists, writers, actors, and other creative types who have stayed or lived there. Among them were William Burroughs, Dylan Thomas, Mark Twain, Eugene O'Neill, Tennessee Williams, Bob Dylan, Thomas Wolfe, Arthur Miller, and O. Henry. Andy Warhol filmed *The Chelsea Girls* there, and several prize-winning works were penned there, including Wolfe's *You Can't Go Home Again* and Miller's *After the Fall.* One musician, Schizo, said that he'd never written before, but at the hotel, he wrote forty songs.

One of the sad stories from this place tells of the slow suicide of Welsh poet Dylan Thomas. In 1953, he went from his rooms to the White Horse Tavern. He claimed that night to have seen the gates of hell and then proceeded to drink 17 shots of whiskey. He made his way back to his room, where he collapsed. He was taken to a hospital, but too late: He died there at the age of 39.

One of the reservation clerks told Katherine that every Halloween the elevator constantly stops at the first floor. That's where the infamous room 100 was located. On October 12, 1978, Sid Vicious, former bass player for the nihilistic London punk group the Sex Pistols, called police to report that someone had stabbed his girlfriend, Nancy Spurgeon. They arrived and found her in her underwear, covered in blood, lying beneath the bathroom sink. She had been stabbed with a hunting knife. Vicious was arrested. He was bailed out, but ended up dead shortly thereafter from a heroin overdose, unwittingly supplied by his own mother.

Hotel Chelsea

Katherine booked a room at the Hotel Chelsea. Her friend, Rosemary, was going to meet her. Rosemary had once resided there and said the hotel housed many ghosts.

She got room 520, a spacious suite with double doors, a kitchenette, two double beds, a round wooden table, an empty bookcase, and a red and black sofa. Over the ornate fireplace was a huge gold-framed mirror, and next to it was an antique dresser with another ornate mirror. She immediately took some photos. Negative. But a little later, she got a photo filled with orbs. Against one purple wall was a rainbow of white bubbles.

The next photo showed less and the third just a few lingering dots on the wall.

Rosemary arrived and lit two tall candles in glass containers, placing one on the floor in a corner and the other on the bookcase. She also lit a small candle that she placed on the table. They should not be blown out, she warned, but gave no explanation about what would happen if they were. Katherine aimed the video camera at the table, shut off the lights, and turned on the infrared. Now it was a waiting game.

Rosemary was hoping to contact her dog, Wizard, who had lived with her in the hotel. The day before he died, Rosemary had taken a photo of him that showed a glowing star over his head. It looked like an orb. She believed he'd come if she called and would be a guide. She tried, but Katherine didn't see any evidence of a ghost dog.

Nothing else happened while Rosemary was there, and after she left, Katherine patiently watched through the video camera for over an hour in the room. She was unable to use it in the hallway to look for Nancy's ghost nearer to where she'd been murdered, because it was brightly lit, with highly reflective white walls.

As Katherine watched through the viewfinder, a sizable orb flew up from her right. Then several orbs came out from under the bed and one bounced along the top of it. She tried to get some EVP but had no luck. If the place was full of ghosts, they weren't in room 520. At least, not with her.

Murder Swamp

In May 1952, Mike Medoved and George Jentsy went out to explore an unnamed island in western Pennsylvania's Beaver River. This general area had eerie connotations from the past. It didn't help the "Murder Swamp's" reputation when they came across a set of ribs and then a leg bone. Both were clearly human. After a bit of digging, they unearthed a skull. Then they went to tell the police.

Four state troopers searched the island, which was just a mile and a half south of where a number of corpses had been discovered in the 1920s and 1930s. They were linked for a while to the Cleveland Torso kills, with a total for both areas of 29 murder-dismemberments. Back then it seemed like they had to be linked for a number of reasons, but more sophisticated profiling today fails to confirm these notions.

The spate of murders, documented in 2013 by James Jessen Badal in his book *Hell's Wasteland*, seemed to begin in 1921, when Emma Jackson was sexually assaulted and nearly beheaded in her own home in Wampum, Pennsylvania, which was close to the railroad tracks. This murder went unsolved. In July 1923, not far away, the badly decomposed body of a 6-year-old girl was found, but she was never identified as a missing child.

In October 1923, a headless nude male corpse was found in a changing shed, near the railroad in south Pittsburgh. Only a couple of photographs offered a lead. Shortly thereafter, some boys found the head about 100 feet from the changing shed. Eventually, this victim was identified as Charles McGregor, a salesman. About three months later, dismembered limbs and a head were found in a burning heap of coal in West Virginia, close to Pittsburgh. There was speculation that the two beheading incidents were linked. Finally, in 1925, a 14-year-old boy was dismembered and burned in a shed, also near railroad tracks, but about 50 miles north of Pittsburgh. None of these murders was solved.

Also in 1925, just a few days apart, the bodies of three different men were discovered in an area across the tracks from New Castle, Pennsylvania, known as "Murder Swamp." Legend had it that organized crime had deposited many victims in that wasteland of small pools and thick undergrowth. For a while, an Italian enforcer organization called The Black Hand had operated in the area, but a series of prosecutions had effectively shut it down.

According to Badal, not much is left of Murder Swamp. A power plant took over most of the land and dirt has filled in most of the bogs. How many bodies were dumped there, undiscovered, is anyone's guess. Some might still be there.

So, back to 1925. In October, the nude, headless body of a young man was found in a sitting position in a depression next to a fallen tree. He'd been covered in several layers of leaves, some of them much fresher than others, as if his killer had returned. Eventually, his head was found buried in a spot where his feet had been. Less than two weeks later, duck hunters turned up another set of male remains.

Two days later, a rabbit hunter came across yet another skeleton near the railroad tracks. This person, whose skull lay 45 feet from the body, had been decapitated. The remains belonged to a middle-aged woman, who appeared to have been strangled by her own belt. The investigators hoped that dental comparisons would help to identify her.

Remains of Torso Killer Victim (Cleveland News)

During this time, dismembered bodies turned up in nearby Cleveland, Ohio. In September 1934, part of a woman's torso, with legs severed at the knees, washed up on the shore of Lake Erie.

A year later in the garbage-strewn area known as Kingsbury Run, two headless mutilated male corpses were found with genitals removed. The younger one was identified as a small-time criminal, and the police dismissed his murder as his just desserts. But then early in 1936, the remains of a prostitute were found in a basket behind a butcher shop, and another decapitated male corpse turned up in Kingsbury Run, inspiring the Cleveland *Plain Dealer* to dub the killer "the Mad Butcher of Kingsbury Run." Two more mutilated bodies turned up, making seven.

The city's Director of Safety was none other than Elliott Ness, former G-man and founder of the Untouchables. He assigned a dozen detectives to the case and burned down the slum from where many victims had come, but corpses continued to show up for two more years. By then the number had reached a dozen, but the killer eluded identification. Ness narrowed in on one suspect, Dr. Francis Edward Sweeney, who then committed himself to a mental hospital and was never proven to be guilty.

Detective Peter Merlyo Undercover

Detective Peter Merlyo stayed on the case until his death in 1947, believing that the killer had actually murdered many more people than the official tally. He was certain that many of the bodies found during the 1920s in "Murder Swamp" were also victims of the Torso Killer's handiwork. The detective thought the killer traveled by boxcar to elude law enforcement and to find victims in other places.

More bodies turned up after the final murder in Cleveland associated with the Mad Butcher (some say there were 12 victims, some say 14). In October 1939, the corpse of a young male surface in Murder Swamp, and then three dismembered bodies, one with carvings on his chest, were found in some boxcars that had come from Youngstown, Ohio, not far from Cleveland. Pittsburgh had its own headless body removed from one of the rivers, along with two human legs found some time later in another river that flowed through the city. Then, another headless corpse.

In a case like this, law enforcement records are crucial. However, Badal has researched the potential links between the Cleveland Torso Killer and the New Castle deaths in Murder Swamp and found a dearth of official records. There was plenty of newspaper coverage, but especially during that era, newspapers published whatever sold papers. Reporters weren't as concerned with the facts.

For forensic purposes, Badal's research is probably the most solid foundation we could have for pondering how to investigate this case. He even looked at a behavioral profile done on the case and accepted that there are links between some of the victims, such as those found in railroad cars, but certainly not all.

The Mad Butcher/Torso Killer has never been officially identified. But people in Cleveland preserve the tale, and some say the ghosts of victims show up in the places where they were found, whether it's in Murder Swamp or other death scene locations. Local folklore even suggests that the Mad Butcher still hunts for victims, restless even in death.

Whatever the case may be, it's certain that a Mad Butcher populates scary tales told to kids, especially those who live where the killer once roamed. Unidentified murderers tend to acquire an immortality that makes them larger than life—especially when remains are found many years later—and scarier.

The Mysterious Death of Frank Smith

We investigated the following incident that took place in the 1980s in the Hotel Bethlehem on Main Street.

Hotel Bethlehem

Frank Smith had a business partnership and kept his office in the hotel. The hotel historian, Natalie Bock, states that Smith had an agreement between himself and his two partners to take out life insurance policies that named each other as beneficiaries. In the event of the death of any one of them, the insurance payout would work as a buy-out of that person's share. The plan had a suicide clause that ran out after two years.

On the Monday following the annual 10-day celebration, Musikfest, which left the street crowded most evenings in front of the hotel, Smith's secretary came in early and saw his jacket lying folded over the back of his chair. She didn't think anything of it and went to breakfast. (One account indicates that she saw him in the dining room at 9:30 A.M., but we could not verify this and it could have been a reporter's misunderstanding.) The secretary reportedly didn't see him the rest of the morning. That afternoon she had to make a copy of something, so she went to the restroom-turned-storage closet where they kept the copy machine. The door was closed and she was unable to open it, so she knocked. No answer. Then she tried pushing on the door, but it seemed to be hindered by something on the other side. The secretary called hotel security.

This man, too, had a difficult time opening the door. Through a crack he could see that Smith's body was up against it. He called the police. To them it appeared that Smith had gone into this small room and shot himself with a .357. However, he had been shot twice—once in the stomach and once in the head. By their best estimates, he had been shot during the fireworks the night before (unless the report of his sighting that morning is correct). This introduced an element of ambiguity, especially when his wife and partners insisted he had not been suicidal.

A few years went by. Around midday one day, a maid saw the figure of a gentleman in a suit, in the bathroom where Smith had died. He disappeared right in front of her. Then an auditor saw the reflection of a man in a glass tabletop on that floor, but no one was there. On this same floor, people have reported the loud crash of weights dropping in the fitness area, when it's locked and no one is inside. This raises questions: is it Frank Smith? Is he trying to get our attention because questions remain about his manner of death?

Forensically, there is no longer any physical evidence, but questioned suicides can be subjected to a psychological autopsy. This involves collecting as much data as possible for a full victimology, which includes their state of mind just prior to the death and using probability analysis along with clinical databases. It would also involve a reconstruction based on crime scene logic.

In death certifications, there are three important matters: the cause, mechanism and manner of death. The cause is an instrument or physical agent used to bring about death (a bullet), the mechanism is the pathological agent in the body that resulted in the death (excessive bleeding), and the manner is considered to be natural, accidental, homicide or suicide. Sometimes the manner isn't clear, so the death is classified as "undetermined."

In such cases, a psychological autopsy might assist the coroner or medical examiner in clearing up the mystery. It involves discovering the state of mind of the victim preceding death. A close examination of the death scene may indicate degree of intent and lethality, and the victimology might identify the details of a suicidal mindset.

Smith was having financial problems and could have been despondent. The civil case offers a few clues. Because the policy's timeframe for no payout in the event of suicide had not expired, Smith's partners went to court with Smith's wife to argue that the death had been an accident. Sally Smith stated that Frank had been in worse financial shape before without talking about or resorting to suicide. He'd left no suicide note. However, they lost their case.

The suicide database tells us that only about one-third of people who kill themselves leave notes. Those who shoot themselves twice generally shoot close to the same place.

Perhaps Smith had tried to stage his suicide to look like a homicide, by shooting himself twice, so that the others could benefit from the policy. We do have a few such suicides on record. But if he had this in mind, it didn't work. The fact that his body blocked the door undermined any such plan.

One other rumor, which was impossible to track down to its source, was that Smith's death had been a contract hit.

However, it would have been difficult for someone to shoot Smith in the bathroom, posed the body against the door as a suicide, and gotten out. (Still, it was not impossible.) It's not clear that any investigation had analyzed the bullet trajectory to see if it could have been self-inflicted.

If Smith is showing up as an apparition, it's possible that he wants his murder to be solved. In addition to theorizing on how a site can be haunted, paranormalists have developed a similar protocol for evaluating why the surviving spirit of a person might remain at a site. In ghost hunting, some of the reasons postulated include: unfinished business; an unexpected death; a youthful death; a violent demise; concern for the living; a death so sudden that they don't know that they're dead; fear of final judgment; and concern that someone among the living is grieving too long. Violent crimes and sudden deaths appear to show up most often in our ghost lore.

With forensics at a dead-end, paranormal methods could assist.

An attempt could be made to collect EVP, asking questions to get a name and perhaps a reason for the haunting. Questions could also help to acquire the death date and possibly something about the circumstances. In addition, using dowsing rods to acquire answers to "yes or no" questions could aid in this endeavor. A psychic could be added as a team member to learn more.

Our team uses three mediums with different strengths—clairvoyance, clairaudience, and an empath. Because Smith apparently shows himself often, this case could be fruitful for a clairvoyant medium to visualize any messages he might be willing to pass on.

In a typical session, we would visit a site where Smith's apparition has been seen and, after a thorough "sweep" of the place with scientific instruments to detect naturally occurring anomalies, ask our medium to see if he is present or to summon him. The medium can then direct to the investigator some questions appropriate for gathering EVP. If Smith is responsive, he can be told that the insurance claim has expired and asked how his death occurred.

While perhaps not germane to solving the case, Smith might be persuaded to have himself filmed on infrared or ultraviolet (digital full spectrum) cameras, or using night vision video cameras. During an interactive session, he might be persuaded to reenact his death, showing whether he killed himself, accidentally shot himself, or was murdered.

An infrared "trail cam" can be set up in the room and left to record any anomalies that occur overnight. This technique had been used successfully in other investigations. Other motion sensing devices can be left, as well as digital recorders set on "Voice Activation" mode to record any anomalous noises. Gunshots have been recorded at certain sites.

During a preliminary investigation using a digital recorder to gather EVP in the room where Smith's body was found, Mark asked if Frank knew what had happened to him. There was a two syllable response, each ending in "er...er." Was it Frank Smith trying to say, "murder?"

Mark Conducting an EVP Session

Katherine persuaded the Northampton County Coroner, Zach Lysek, to pull the original case files. He thought the bullet trajectories were odd for a suicide. There were two .380 slugs to the chest (not one to the leg, as reported in the newspaper). One trajectory was downward and one was at an upward angle. They were non-contact wounds, so the gun muzzle had been 6-12 inches from the wounds. There was no gunshot residue on Smith's hands, and one spent bullet was found in Smith's bag. The pathologist stated that there had been an odd residue found on Smith.

In addition, Lysek learned that a shot had been fired into Smith's house not long before, into his son's bedroom. This is the type of thing someone in organized crime might do as a warning. He wanted to pull up a confidential file to see what Smith's wife had actually said at the federal hearing, as well as to see if she was still alive and might talk with him. As of this writing, no further work had been done. So far, there was no evidence that Smith had been depressed and no substances, such as antidepressants, were found in his body.

The Three Babes

In November 1934, just after the kidnapping and murder of Charles Lindbergh, Jr., two men were driving on Rt. 233 on South Mountain in Pennsylvania's Cumberland County to cut firewood. They spotted a green blanket in the woods. Curious, they walked over and picked it up, only to discover that it covered the bodies of three dead children. Dressed in coats with fur collars, one was snuggled into the arms of a second one, while the third lay close by. The men ran to get help.

The Carlisle police processed the scene and speculated that, from their looks, they were probably sisters. Still, there were no leads. Five days later, a black leather suitcase turned up five miles away. It contained a notebook. Inside, in a child's scribble, was the name, "Norma." On the same day, the bodies of a young couple were found at a deserted railroad flag-stop in Altoona. Both had been shot. A few more days passed before an abandoned 1929 blue Pontiac sedan was located at a lovers' lane in Mifflin County. It had California license plates.

The dead man, it turned out, was Elmo Noakes. Yet this did not establish any connection between him and the dead girls. An autopsy indicated that they had been strangled and asphyxiated. They'd also been starving.

A public viewing was set up in Carlisle, drawing thousands of curious people, including parents of missing children. No one could identify them. However, a bus driver recalled a woman with three children boarding the bus. She had a black leather suitcase. They'd come from New York. It was a false lead.

A restaurant owner in Philadelphia reported that a family had come in recently. The man was looking for work. He mentioned that his children had become a "burden." Noakes had family in California who recalled that he'd purchased a Pontiac sedan. The next day, the entire family had vanished. His daughters were Norma, 12, Dewilla, 10, and Cordelia, 8. Noakes' 18-year-old niece, Winifred Pierce, had also disappeared. Noakes' wife had died two years earlier and his niece had moved in with him.

As detectives pieced together their travels, it seemed that they had used fictitious names to move around. Noakes was unable to find work. Eventually, he had killed his daughters, leaving them in the woods, and had driven the car until it ran out of gas. He and his niece then hitchhiked to Altoona. There, Winifred pawned her coat and Noakes purchased a .22-caliber rifle for $2.85. This he used to kill them both.

A large blue and gold sign near the site of where the girls had died says simply, "On this spot were found three babes in the woods Nov.– 24 –1934." Some say that paranormal phenomena are experienced here and in the cemetery where they are buried. Supposedly, the girls cry for their mother.

A week before Halloween 2013, Mark was in Carlisle to deliver a speech. On their way, Mark and Carol stopped at Westminster Cemetery, where the Babes in the Woods are buried, to do a short preliminary paranormal investigation on the case.

(Despite popular belief, cemeteries are not the ideal place to conduct a paranormal investigation. First, most people in the field—from professional paranormal investigators to theologians over the millennia—agree that the body has little to do with the spirit or soul. As one sage put it, we are souls carrying around corpses. Put it this way: When you die, are you going to want to hang around your decomposing body? Second, if spirits do hang around cemeteries, they would have a tendency to contaminate whatever evidence the investigator got. How are you to know to whom you are speaking when there are potentially thousands of spirits in the cemetery? Nevertheless, we were in the area and we considered it a preliminary investigation with the potential to visit the drop off site, or perhaps the murder site later.)

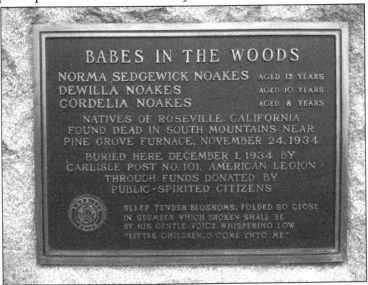

BABES IN THE WOODS
NORMA SEDGEWICK NOAKES AGED 12 YEARS
DEWILLA NOAKES AGED 10 YEARS
CORDELIA NOAKES AGED 8 YEARS
NATIVES OF ROSEVILLE, CALIFORNIA
FOUND DEAD IN SOUTH MOUNTAINS NEAR
PINE GROVE FURNACE, NOVEMBER 24, 1934
BURIED HERE DECEMBER 1, 1934 BY
CARLISLE POST NO. 101, AMERICAN LEGION
THROUGH FUNDS DONATED BY
PUBLIC-SPIRITED CITIZENS
SLEEP TENDER BLOSSOMS, FOLDED SO CLOSE
IN SLUMBER WHICH BROKEN SHALL BE
BY HIS GENTLE VOICE WHISPERING LOW
"LITTLE CHILDREN, O COME UNTO ME"

We took photos at the gravesite. Unfortunately, no images were captured in the short amount of time allotted to the investigation. An attempt at obtaining EVP was made. Both photos and recordings were inconclusive.

Jailhouse Spirits

One of the more picturesque places in Northern Virginia is a small village, restored and preserved, apparently frozen in nineteenth-century time: Brentsville.

Near the famed battlefields of Manassas—and even closer to the not-so-well-known battlefield of Bristoe Station—it was established in 1820 as the county seat of Prince William County. In 1893, the county seat moved to Manassas, and the town of Brentsville, with no reason to modernize, retained its nineteenth-century rural ambience.

Currently the site embraces 28 acres and includes the restored 1822 courthouse and jail, the Haislip-Hall House, the Union Church, a one-room schoolhouse and the Brentsville Tavern, currently undergoing an archaeological investigation. For our purposes, consider the courthouse and the jail.

Former Prince William County Courthouse

According to L. B. Taylor in his book *The Big Book of Virginia Ghost Stories* (Stackpole Books), employees at the Brentsville Courthouse Historic Centre have had bizarre and unexplainable events happen to them in both buildings. Their website even admits the presence of the ghost of the "mad man of the Brentsville jail." Local ghost hunting groups have gathered physical evidence during several investigations of the site: EVP of an angry voice shouting, "Get out! Get out of here!" and a second voice pleading, "Don't turn out the lights!" An investigator had a reel of fishing line tossed at him by invisible hands. Shadow people have been seen moving swiftly around the complex. The Brentsville Historical Courthouse Centre has decided to embrace their ghosts rather than deny them and, in October, holds haunted jail tours.

Certainly jails and courthouses hold the remnant energies of those supremely agitated souls who disappointed both themselves and their fellow citizens during their lives. Not only were there those who learned of their imminent incarceration in the courthouse, then served that confinement in the jail, but there were those ultimate criminals who sat out the last miserable minutes of their lives in the jail before the final arbiter—the hangman—set them free.

But it seems that even death did not free all of them, for many appear to be trapped within the confines of the 28 acres of old Brentsville.

Taylor writes that in 1839 a slave was hanged for setting a fire in the jail. Then, in 1845, a slave named Katy murdered a landowner named Gerald Mason. She was tried in the courthouse, imprisoned in the jail, and executed for her deed. In 1856, five slaves were involved in the killing of George E. Green, their master. Nelly appeared to be the ringleader; they entered Green's house where she slammed an ax into him. Green ran for his life and the rest pursued, beating him with the ax, sticks and other farm implements. They dragged him into the house and set it on fire. His terror must have been unimaginable. When asked their motive, the perpetrators claimed he was a hard master, starving them, failing to provide clothing and not allowing them to attend meetings.

After the trial, Nelly, who had confessed to the crime, and two others were executed. The other two were pardoned because of "their youth and feeble intellect."

As if that wasn't enough to cause spirits to remain, in 1872, Prince William County's commonwealth attorney, James F. Clark was accused of kidnapping and seducing Fannie Fewell, the beautiful 16-year-old daughter of a prominent local family. Though claiming innocence, Clark was tossed into the Brentsville jail to await justice.

Enter Lucien (Rhoda) Fewell, Fannie's brother who came all the way from Lynchburg to avenge his sister's honor. Either someone had made sure the guards were taken care of or Lucien was supremely fortunate, because when he arrived at the jail it was unlocked and there was not a deputy in sight.

He casually strolled into the jail and asked the only other person present, a boy, which cell was Clark's. Pointed in the right direction, he drew a pistol and fired at the helpless lawyer through the bars. Two shots missed, and when he thrust the weapon through the bars for a better shot, Clark grabbed it. The whole story might have a different ending if Clark had wrestled the gun away from Lucien. As it happened, the vengeful brother was well armed that day. He pulled another gun from a pocket and put a bullet into Clark's chest. He calmly walked out of the jail leaving the accused dead on his cell floor.

Eppa Hunton, formerly a general in Robert E. Lee's Army of Northern Virginia, defended Fewell. His plea to Southern manhood, which apparently allowed the cold-blooded murder of a man who soiled the honor of a young maiden, fell on welcome ears; a jury, which had deliberated all of five minutes, found Fewell not guilty. Northern papers declared the verdict a travesty of justice.

Could some of the paranormal activity be caused by Clark's unhappy spirit? Could Clark have been wrongly accused?

In August 2009, the investigators from TAPS visited Brentsville Courthouse Historic Centre to investigate the claims of eyewitnesses who saw faces peering from the courthouse windows, particularly from the window of the judge's room on the second floor. The face of an African

American woman has been seen at the jailhouse door, and then it vanishes.

Jason and Grant of the TAPS team investigated the jail and captured an indistinct image on their thermal camera. On the second floor they heard footsteps moving around in the room next to them. A check with the infrared camera revealed no one there. Although the jail has no electricity running into it, according to the Brentsville site manager, the TAPS team got spikes on an EMF meter and heard knocking. Through the knocking they apparently communicated with an entity.

The TAPS investigation of the courthouse drew no results.

Yet there are the persistent sightings by locals of apparitions walking around the buildings and disembodied voices being heard in the jail.

Starvation Heights

During the turn of the nineteenth century and into the early years of the twentieth, spas for the wealthy that purported to "cure" people of contemporary ills were all the rage. Some offered genuine service, but a few were full of quackery, poised simply to siphon off money from trusting clients. Kenneth V. Iserson, in *Demon Doctors*, and Gregg Olsen, in *Starvation Heights*, offer an account of a female doctor who used her "medicine" for sinister ends.

Dr. Linda Burfield Hazzard set up her operation in 1907 in Seattle, Washington, and offered several versions of a published manual of her special method. Trained as an osteopath, she presented herself as the only licensed fasting therapist in the country, and her final domain was a sanitarium, Wilderness Heights, in the small town of Olalla, across the Puget Sound from Seattle.

It was an isolated place, with no direct way to communicate with the outside world. Exuding self-confidence, Dr. Hazzard assured people that her method was a panacea for all manner of ills, because she was able to rid the body of toxins that supposedly caused imbalances. As strange as it may seem, she managed to persuade people to go without food, aside from some water and a thin tomato and asparagus soup, for long periods of time. As their bodies shed "toxins," she required enemas (a fashionable purgative in many such places) and provided vigorous massages meant to accelerate the process.

As patients weakened, Hazzard found ways to encourage them to turn over to her their accounts and power of attorney. Not surprisingly, several died under her "care" and she grew richer. Her bigamous husband, Sam, helped get the patients, once they were very weak, to change their wills to make Dr. Hazzard their beneficiary. Yet when attacked for her methods as patients died, she insisted that they had been near death when they came, and she could not be expected to work miracles. Even with these dire stories, she still drew both disciples and patients from around the world. Local residents dubbed the place Starvation Heights, and it caught the attention of authorities when two wealthy British sisters came to "take the cure."

Sisters Claire and Dora Williamson had received a copy of *Fasting for the Cure of Disease*, Hazzard's publication. It purported to have effected remarkable recoveries for people who had found little help elsewhere. Hazzard's ideas spread to an international audience. She had published testimonials from success stories, and the sisters were impressed. A fan of natural cures, they checked in for the treatment on February 27, 1911.

They did not realize that, once there, they would not be able to leave. In fact, they would be too weak to do so. They agreed to undergo the rigorous fasting, shedding weight to the point where they were nearly mere skeletons. As they grew weaker, Olson points out, they became more committed to the therapy. Suffering was a sign, they were told, that the treatment was working. Even when they became bedridden after two months, the doctor would not allow them to eat. At the same time, she secured their jewelry and land deeds, to "prevent others" from coming into their apartment to rob them. Then she moved them to her newly completed sanitarium, where they could communicate with no one. At that time, they weighed around 75 pounds each and were often delirious.

In secret, Claire managed to persuade someone to send a telegram, but she died, even as Margaret Convey, a faithful nanny, rushed there from Australia. Convey rescued Dora, now said to be insane, before she met the same fate. Dora had endured the treatment for four months, but with Convey's help, she regained her health. When the case came to trial in 1912, Dora was an effective witness—especially when jurors saw the disturbing photos of her during the latter stage of the fasting cure. Hazzard was found guilty of manslaughter. The medical establishment removed her license during the legal proceedings, and she claimed that the verdict was part of the mainstream persecution she'd suffered all along.

During her appeal, two women died at her center.

Hazzard spent only two years in prison, and in exchange for her leaving the country, the governor granted a pardon. She went to New Zealand, but eventually returned to Olalla and resumed her treatments. Arrested again when another man died, she was fined for violating medical practice. Since she kept no records, the number of people who died (or were intentionally starved to death) under her "care" cannot be estimated. Some say 12 and others place it at 40.

The sanitarium eventually burned down and Hazzard expired on the property three years later. Apparently, she was trying to cure herself with her own fasting treatment. The cottage where she had lived has changed hands a few times.

The family who lived there during the 1990s experienced some paranormal phenomena. Once, the woman was in the kitchen, cooking. She moved back and forth between a counter on her left and the stove. When she turned around, she saw that every chair in the kitchen, and a few from the room next door, had been piled up against the bathroom door, which was on the opposite side of the room. No one else was home.

In the attic were several low ledges. A psychic who visited the place said she saw the spirits of Hazzard's victims sitting on them. The psychic sensed great anguish in this space.

Washington State Paranormal Investigations and Research (WSPIR) visited Starvation Heights three times. Each of the teams included a psychic who'd been kept in the dark about their destination. On the way there, two of them sensed they were on their way to a large medical type of institution. One psychic found a book on the stairs that Hazzard had written, but the homeowners swore they had hidden it away to avoid tainting the visions. Several teams got EVP that they said were "Help me" and other phrases that had no real significance, except for "Dig us up."

During an overnight investigation, one team member chose to stay in the room in which Hazzard had died. He reportedly entered a trance state and answered simple questions with rumbles of "yes" or "no." Other team members thought he was communicating with Linda Hazzard, as if she did not want to leave the place.

The TV show "The Dead Files" also filmed an episode featuring Starvation Heights.

The cottage was demolished when the family moved into a new home they had built elsewhere on the property.

Jack the Ripper

Although this book is about haunted crime scenes in the United States, we've included the section on Jack the Ripper for a couple of reasons. First, several suspects thought to be the Ripper journeyed to America after the murders in London stopped. *The Discovery Channel* even ran a program considering the possibility that Jack had relocated his grisly hobby to these shores.

Secondly, the United States is not the only place where there are crime scenes haunted by victims and others associated with the crime. We intend to include some of the international haunted crime scenes in the third in this series.

Ripper Street

The murders attributed to the person called Jack the Ripper seemed to begin in August 1888, with Mary Ann "Polly" Nichols, killed on Friday, August 31, just after 1:00 A.M. She was 42, alcoholic, a mother of five, and a prostitute. (Some Ripperologists place the start of this series earlier in August, with victim Martha Tabram, also fatally knifed 39 times. There were some differences between these attacks, but it's difficult in retrospect to ignore the pattern of the dates.) As Polly went out to earn money for lodging, someone grabbed her and slit her throat with two powerful strokes. When found at 3:40 in the morning in a stable entrance on Buck's Row, (which is now Durward Street), she was on her back, her skirt was pulled up to her waist and her legs were parted. She'd been cut ear to ear, all the way to the spinal cord, nearly severing her head from her body. On the left side of the neck, just below the jaw, a four-inch long incision started at the ear. The second cut ran to eight inches. There was a circular bruise on the left side of the face, perhaps from the pressure of fingers, and on the lower part of the abdomen, there was a deep and jagged wound.

Polly's ghost reportedly appears in this area, sometimes lying on the ground where the body was dropped.

Site of Polly Nichols Murder

The next "official" Ripper victim was prostitute Annie Chapman, 45. Her body was discovered on the morning of September 8, thirty minutes after she'd last been seen alive, behind a lodging house on Hanbury Street. This is a few blocks from where Polly was killed. Her dress had been pulled over her head, her stomach ripped open, and her small intestine pulled out and draped over her right shoulder. Two flaps of skin from the lower abdomen lay above the left shoulder. Her face was smeared with blood. Her legs were drawn up, knees bent and spread outward, with her feet flat on the ground. Her jaw was bruised and her throat was cut twice in a jagged manner, from left to right and back again, and quite deep. The weapon was probably a surgical type of knife with a narrow blade. In addition, Annie's protruding tongue indicated asphyxiation.

Since there was no sign of a struggle, aside from blood about fourteen inches high on a nearby fence, it seemed that she'd been quickly subdued. A pocket carried under her skirt had been cut open at the front and side, and a comb and paper case lay close by. Some pennies, two new farthings, and two rings from her fingers had been arranged at her feet and a closer inspection showed that her pelvis, two-thirds of the bladder, half of the vagina, and the uterus had been removed. An envelope stamped London, August 1888, bore the letter 'M' and a seal from the Sussex regiment was found nearby. It's not clear how any of these items was related to the murder.

This area, too, gets reports of sudden screams in the night, as if a woman is being violated. (However, it is a very busy area, with a lot of residences cramped together.) Some people claim to have seen a female apparition dressed in clothing from the Ripper era, and her head rests on her shoulder, as if she cannot use her neck.

Back to 1888. By the end of that month, on September 30, there were two victims on the same night, within a fifteen-minute walk of each other. At #60 Berner Street, someone slashed the throat of Elizabeth Stride, 45, only a few minutes before she was found. Less than an hour later, Catherine Eddowes was killed in Mitre Square and disemboweled. (Despite how close these scenes are, it requires crossing a very public main street, and some Ripperologists understandably have decided that Stride is *not* a Ripper victim. Katherine visited the area and had doubts herself. It could be that two women were killed in unrelated incidents on the same night.)

Eddowes lay on her back with her left leg extended and her right bent. Her arms were straight by her sides, palms upward, and she had been cut from the rectum to the breastbone, with her intestine pulled out and placed over her right shoulder. It was smeared with an unusual substance and a two-foot piece had been cut and placed along the left side of the body. The left kidney had also been removed and was missing, and the victim's face was oddly mutilated. Two upside-down Vs were cut into her cheeks, pointing toward the eyes, her eyelids were nicked, and the tip of her nose was cut off. One earlobe was also clipped. And, as with the other victims her throat was slashed with a six-inch cut. However, the blood had not spurted. In fact, she'd been cut several times through her clothing, which had caught much of the blood. A bloodstained apron was tied around her neck. (In contrast, hardly anything beyond a cut to the throat was done to Stride. Maybe the killer was interrupted, as some theorists believe, or maybe it was a different killer.)

Apparitions have been seen in both locations, along with reports of the sounds of agonized groaning.

After the autopsy, police found part of the apron that had been tied around Eddowes' neck lying a third of a mile away from the murder scene, with apparent stains from a knife being wiped on it. Nearby, a message was written on a wall, "The Juwes are not the men that will be blamed for nothing." (No one knows if the message was written that night or some other time.)

Catherine Eddowes Murder Site

Two weeks after the "double event" came a letter and box "from Hell" to the head of the Whitechapel Vigilance Committee, with a grisly trophy: half of a kidney preserved in wine. By some accounts, the organ turned out to have been from someone afflicted with Bright's disease—a disorder from which Eddowes (and many other prostitutes) was believed to have suffered. The note's author indicated that he'd fried and eaten the other half, which was "very nise." It was believed that this note was from the killer (if not a pranking medical student) and he even offered to send "the bloody knife" in due time. He closed with the taunt, "Catch me if you can." No knife was forthcoming.

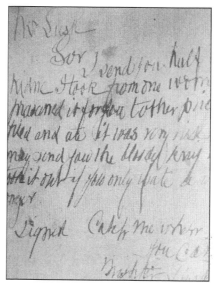

On November 8, the Ripper apparently went after Mary Kelly, 24. She lived with a man with whom she frequently quarreled. Kelly drank heavily. On the night of her murder, she had invited a man to her rented room at Miller's Court Spitalfields (adjacent to Whitechapel). The man seen was short and stout, with a blotchy face and mustache. It's not clear whether he was her killer, because another witness said he saw Kelly later with a well-dressed man with a mustache with whom she seemed friendly. He was in his mid-thirties and reportedly had a Jewish appearance.

Probably around 4:00 A.M., the man with Kelly pulled the sheet over her head to stab her through it. Then he slashed open her throat, ripped her lower torso, cut off both breasts, skinned the forehead, pulled out her intestines, and skinned her chest and legs, spattering blood all over the room. The left arm and head hung from the body by the skin only.

When police arrived the following morning, they found a severed breast on the bed table, decorated with the tips of her nose and ears in the mocking rendition of a face. The reeking contents of her abdomen were spread over the bed and thrown around the room. The liver was between her feet. Her heart was missing and flesh had been cut from her legs and buttocks clear to the bone. One of her hands was pushed into her open stomach. Doctors who were called to the scene estimated that this frenzy had gone on for at least two hours. The victim's clothing lay folded neatly on a chair, and other clothing had been burned in the grate—a skirt and a hat. Kelly's remains were so mutilated the police had to use a butcher's tray to remove them from the premises.

This building no longer stands. It's been demolished since the Ripper days, yet people claim to see a female face looking out a window. (Katherine has been there, and did not find a building with a window that would support such reports.) They also describe a figure dressed in old-fashioned black garb entering the building that now stands there.

All of the Ripper's victims would be considered high-risk, in that they were all desperately poor prostitutes with drinking problems who plied their trade in and around the same pubs and on the same streets of the crime-ridden Whitechapel area. All were around 40-years-of-age except Mary Kelly. Like numerous other serial killers, Jack the Ripper seems to have been motivated, at least in part, by a tortured sexual pathology. Prostitutes were logical targets.

Jack the Ripper was, in all probability, a single white male who lived alone in the Whitechapel area. This allowed him to come home after a murder without having to answer any questions about where he'd been, what he'd been doing, and why he and his clothing were bloody. He probably drank and ate in the same local pubs as did his victims and might have been acquainted with them. Perhaps he was a former customer. He was nocturnal and prowled his Whitechapel neighborhood on a regular basis.

Ten Bells Pub

The Ten Bells Pub across the Spitalfields Market area in Whitechapel, where Catherine Eddowes and Mary Kelly hung out, is said to be haunted. Some residents of apartments over the pub claimed to have had run-ins with an older man in Victorian clothing. Sometimes he would even lie down beside them on the bed. Some residents felt invisible hands pushing them from behind or heard footsteps when no one was there. In 2000, a pub owner who found a box of items deduced that the male figure was a prior owner, George Roberts, who'd been murdered.

Ivor Edwards's 2003 book, *Jack the Ripper's Black Magic Rituals*, claims that "Jack" was Robert D'Onston Stephenson, a magician/surgeon and possible wife-killer with a clear sense of purpose, an understanding of geographical geometry, and the graceful movements of a cat. Edwards says that drawing lines on a map from one murder site to the next forms a clear occult pattern.

Australian Spiro Dimolianis makes a more careful study. He combed through infamous occultist Aleister Crowley's autobiography, which offered a dramatic rendering of Stephenson as the Magician/Ripper. Supposedly, Stephenson believed he could acquire the power of invisibility by sacrificing seven women in a star pattern. As Dimolianis lays out the general *zeitgeist*, with reliance on psychics, mediums, and their ilk, he demonstrates how the Ripper's spree gave rise to the myth that the Devil, himself, walked the Whitechapel streets.

Jack the Ripper was never caught.

While evidence obtained through paranormal means is currently not admissible in a court of law in the United States, many crime scene investigators are happy to take new leads from any source they can—including PFIs: Paranormal Forensic Investigators. The leads may not pan out, but not all the leads from eyewitnesses bring convictions and what was once cutting-edge forensic science—like lie detectors and hair analysis—have proven just as fallible as anything gleaned paranormally. Perhaps by working together, CSIs and PFIs will someday solve crimes or cold cases hitherto thought unsolvable.

Acknowledgments

Katherine and Mark would like to thank to those who assisted with information and support: Laine Crosby, Dana DeVito, Shannon Frost-Holzemer, Rosemary Ellen Guiley, Colleen Keller, Zack Lysek, Gregg McCrary, Holly Martin, Ruth and Doug Osborne, Dave Pauly, Ingrid Pochron, Patty Wilson, The Lizzie Borden House and Staff, the Hotel Bethlehem and Staff, and especially our editor, Carol Nesbitt.

Katherine also wishes to thank Sally Keglovitz for proof reading the first draft, and for being such an enthusiastic fan of the project.

About the Authors

Dr. Katherine Ramsland has published more than 1,000 articles and 52 books, including *Blood & Ghosts, The Forensic Psychology of Criminal Minds, The Ivy League Killer, Psychopath, The Human Predator, Inside the Minds of Serial Killers*, and *The Mind of a Murderer*. She holds graduate degrees in forensic psychology, clinical psychology, criminal justice, and philosophy, and teaches forensic psychology and criminal justice at DeSales University in Pennsylvania. Ramsland has worked with prominent criminalists, coroners, detectives, and FBI profilers. She speaks internationally about forensic psychology and serial murder, and has appeared on numerous documentaries, as well as *The Today Show, 20/20, 48 Hours, Nancy Grace, Larry King Live* and *E! True Hollywood Story.* She also writes a blog, Shadow Boxing, for *Psychology Today.*

Mark Nesbitt was a National Park Service Ranger/Historian for five years at Gettysburg before starting his own research and writing company. Since then he has published over fifteen books, including *Blood & Ghosts, Civil War Ghost Trails, The Ghost Hunters Field Guide: Gettysburg & Beyond*, and the national award-winning *Ghosts of Gettysburg* series. His stories have been seen on *The History Channel, A&E, The Discovery Channel, The Travel Channel, Unsolved Mysteries,* and numerous regional television shows and heard on *Coast to Coast AM*, and regional radio. In 1994, he created the commercially successful *Ghosts of Gettysburg Candlelight Walking Tours*®, and in 2006, the *Ghosts of Fredericksburg Tours.*

Connect with **Katherine Ramsland** on Social Media:
www.katherineramsland.com
facebook.com/katherine.ramsland
twitter.com/KatRamsland
psychologytoday.com/blog/shadow-boxing
goodreads.com/author/show/24645.Katherine_Ramsland

Connect with **Mark Nesbitt** on Social Media:
facebook.com/mark.v.nesbitt
twitter.com/hauntgburg
markvnesbitt.wordpress.com
foursquare.com/hauntgburg
goodreads.com/author/show/19835.Mark_Nesbitt

Join the ***Haunted Crime Scenes*** conversation:
www.facebook.com/hauntedcrimescenes
hauntedcrimescenes@gmail.com

Made in the USA
Lexington, KY
15 December 2015